A CATECHISM
FOR THE
CHILDREN OF DE-LIGHT

by

Harry MacCormack

A Catechism for the Children of De-Light

Publisher's Cataloging-in-Publication
(Provided by Quality Books, Inc.)

MacCormack, Harry, 1942-
    A catechism for the children of De-Light / by Harry
MacCormack. -- 1st ed.
    p. cm.
    "A sunbow book."
    LCCN 2001090496
    ISBN 0-9649573-2-9

    1. Deep ecology--Philosophy. 2. Human ecology--
Philosophy. 3. Metaphysics. I. Title.

GE195.M33 2001   179'.1
                              QB101-700622

A *Sunbow Book*
Published by *Touchstone Adventures*
ISBN: 0-9649573-2-9
Library of Congress Control Number: 2001090496

A Catechism for the Children of De-Light

Books by Harry MacCormack

Poetry —
Frost for Our Panes
Call of the Mountains
The Displaced Warrior

Other —
The Transition Document:
   Toward An Environmentally Sound Agriculture

Hexagram 46 - Shêng / Pushing Upward

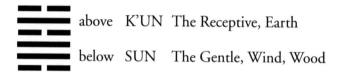 above   K'UN   The Receptive, Earth

below   SUN   The Gentle, Wind, Wood

"…just as a plant needs energy for pushing upward
through the earth."

The hexagram above is what, when consulted in regard to
A Catechism for the Children of Delight, the ancient Chinese
Oracle, the *I Ching* (or *Book of Changes*), had to 'say.'
— Richard Wilhelm translation from Chinese to German,
rendered into English by Cary F. Baynes —

Table of Contents

A Catechism for the Children of De-Light

A Catechism for the Children of De-Light

~ x ~

Introductions

A Catechism for the Children of De-Light

~ How we choose to walk indicates our humanness. We are signs of ourselves and of the whole universe. Each moment we make decisions either to be one with the totality or go on with the attempt to "live" as fragments. This book explores the complexity of conscious, moment-to-moment awareness.

Harry and I go way back in years of brotherhood. While I was working on *Seven Arrows* we discussed our mutual tasks of making Spirit manifest in our consumer world. I have traveled all over the planet visiting with elders in many cultures. What we've shared is an inherited sense of natural orientation, of four directions, supported by the various stories, which embody the history of who we are rather than who we want to be. Harry, as a spirit warrior, has taken those same sensibilities and attempted to change the destructive directions modern society promotes. I've watched him introduce the principles written in this *Catechism* to students, into business, and in his work to bring about an environmentally sound agriculture.

This book, this look at the nature of and importance of the stories that we tell, is meant to help in our awakening. As a reader of this book chances are that you have received "education" in higher institutions of learning. You are also probably aware that we are at a major crossroads regarding human interactions with all life on this planet. This book gives voice to the nature of our mutual quandaries. It also points toward a way for us to conceive of and live our wholeness. Harry would never have written this book was it not for perceptions formed while story-telling among our indigenous culture. He also would not have so clearly framed the contrasts between dominant and pagan consciousness had he not absorbed the best of Western education. Many, many of us share this kind of half-breed conceptual consciousness. This book guides us in the critical task of being alert to the intricate dimensionality of our awareness so that we can regain collective decision-making, not as isolated humans, but in a shared consort with all life on this earth. ~

Hyemeyhosts Storm

A Catechism for the Children of De-Light

~ There were many things in this book that hit a responsive chord with me. Some of the points made me smile with the recognition of similar things that have happened in my life, some sections I read carefully—deciding to try what was being outlined—while for others—not familiar with the territory being covered—I thought that I needed a better map, a more definitive explanation. But then it struck me that this book was not meant to be a map, but rather something to tweak your interest in taking the journey.

Every journey begins long before you put that first foot on the road. It actually begins when you first begin to conceptualize that a journey is needed, that there's going to be a road in your future. Like most humans, I am more comfortable with a guidebook, I like to have at least one hand held. But, as with most journeys in my life that were worth taking, there is no guide to this journey. Harry's role is not that of the scarecrow in the Wizard of Oz, who asks if you are going one way or the other, and then proceeds to journey with you down the road. Harry is answering a few questions, setting the stage for that journey, not giving you a step-by-step description of the journey and what to expect and when to expect it.

I work with the interactions of soil organisms, an area of science that, until recently, most people were either unaware or wildly misinformed. We have begun to understand the Soil Foodweb, which properly managed, can reduce the use of pesticides and inorganic fertilizers. And in order to do this we need the presence of beneficial bacteria, fungi, protozoa, nematodes and microarthropods in the soil.

But the "stories" told in the popular press represent the organisms in the soil as being dangerous, unclean, and unhealthy. They are things we should fear. Advertisements on TV tell us the organisms on our bodies are odor-causing, and deodorants are needed to protect us from their handiwork. The bacteria in our mouths need to be destroyed with bad-breath-fighting toothpaste or mouthwash. Our hands have "germs" on them and we have to use antibacterial soap in order to safeguard our families, our children. Horrors that the baby should encounter a "germ"!

The popular mythology about these organisms is an example of an important theme in this book. We have vilified a whole group of organisms, most of which are beneficial to us, in order to sell products. The truth, however, has little to do with these myths. These stories—the way the concepts are stated, the subtle clues used to tell us these critters are bad—exemplify our use of language to make something into that which it is not.

We need to give soil life the recognition it deserves. We need, as a basic priority, to bring the vibrant lives of microbes—their multifaceted stories—to the decision-making table as part of the basis from which we operate. We need to change our paradigm so we can realize what we can and can not allow, as well as what we have to do. How we interact with microbial life, how we sustain that life, while utilizing the vital resources of soil, air, and water requires a different kind of thought process. Reorienting our speech, being aware that it is our words which allows us to creatively expand or promote destruction, is quite a task. Science may provide the hard data on which to base decisions, on which to build our stories, but the decisions about how to act depends so very often on the speech we use to justify the actions. How we interpret facts and more importantly, how we bring our perceptions into that interpretation, is critically important.

Bio-energy fields are fascinating to me—life resonates at several different frequencies. Cell, tissue, organ, individual, each has its unique frequency signature. At a practical level, a compost or tea which is most bio-active is most likely to be able to maintain that bioactivity. Applying this understanding we watch health return to the soil on a daily basis. We need to promote a language that recognizes the value in the health of the soil. Part of the benefit of reading this book is increased awareness of the principles that would support this needed shift, a turning-around, of our most fundamental perceptions. ⌒

Elaine Ingham

A Catechism for the Children of De-Light

A Few Words for the Poet

⌒ Duality is a prison. You end up hating yourself. It destroys worlds. The ego lays wasteland to reality.

"There must be some way out of here..."
— Bob Dylan —

Vanity and vexation of the spirit. We are not our bodies though we inhabit them with differing degrees of awareness, like the 21,600 daily breaths that occupy our attention, to some degree, sometimes, during the years of our lives.

High density smartness, a level beady eye towards problems and their resolution, trapped in words when the problems transcend thought, grappling with the ego-dominant and eco-destructive behavior of our species, Harry MacCormack, engages head-on with many of the primary philosophical and historical paradigms that sew us up, web us in and pack us up as another to-be-pruned branch of the tree of life.

Harry would give us another fate.

Atropos, one of the fates, as nightshades, puts us to sleep with stars in our eyes. Coming from montane Bolivia, potatoes gave soft food to toothless people and have led to the continuing bestowal of foodplants for humanity developed by heathens/pagans/natives. Now corporate industry wants to own them, and their genes as well. Only nature outwits the vain.

"The bigger they are, the harder they fall, one and all..."
— Bob Marley —

Plants are more complicated than animals. Rice has 50,000 genes, humans 32,000, fruit flies 14,400, coliform bacteria 2000, f2 bacterial virus has three. Mathematics is all nice and sweet but biological life is the center of the earthworld we now inhabit.

A-light, B-light, C-light, De-light, cognitive levels of the divine illumination that informs us about ourselves, the superuniverses of time in space, as we garden biodiversity while Harry reaches beyond the veils to integrate a transcendental view of where we are and how we can grow out of our limitations.

A Catechism for the Children of De-Light

Still more people are needed on the highway of diamonds. Exercising his wit, organic farmer, playwright and outspoken critic of the status quo, Harry invites us to compost our schizophrenias in the garden of unity. He gives recipes.

Violence is as old as the food system. Predation dates to bacteria. We, however, have an alternative, and there are examples. Rosaceaous fruits; nourishing, delicious, hardy in the temperate zone: cherries, apples, plums, peaches, apricots, pears allow us food and nonviolent food if we replant the seeds. Cucurbits, eat the pulp and save the seeds. Avocados, citrus, and in the roots, yacon, the Andean high inulin root related to dahlias, sunflowers and Jerusalem artichokes. Why is it a nonviolent foodcrop? Because the central crown contains the eyes used to propagate more plants while the lateral tubers (up to 2-3 pounds) have no eyes and are solely food.

Protein synthesis, the cellular ability to make proteins of unique sequences of amino acids following nucleic acid taped instructions has provided humanity a model for precision building at the molecular and cellular levels. We must be careful how we use this discovery. Nanotechnology, like molecular biology and perhaps, unfortunately, like atomic energy has great promise and profound dangers.

As an alien species, we divide and conquer. As parents we nurture and circumstance initiations into greater insight and self-realization. Linear is limited. An infinite universe has other designs as well. Beyond the senses is a great mystery. Only occasionally is it rational. All of us have a piece of it. Yoga stills the mind to find it. Legion is its name. ⟶

Alan Kapuler

A Catechism for the Children of De-Light

⌒ When Harry and I were having a discussion some years ago about the sort of issues raised in this book I said to him "you can't have it both ways." He has told me that these words guided the writing you are about to read.

As a child I was taken from my native home and placed in boarding school. The nuns cut our hair and forbid us to speak in our indigenous languages. Our culture, our ceremonies, our way of being with Mother Earth was to be replaced with Christianity and Industrial greed. I survived this ordeal and have remained a Sundancer; a protector of my people's ancient traditions. Yet I am a woman educated by the dominant culture with a Bachelor of Fine Arts (BFA). I live surrounded by the trappings of consumerism. Harry and I have talked about this situation a lot. Much of what you are about to experience in this book is the essence of those discussions. My run for governor of Minnesota in 1990 was an attempt to alert the general public to the type of conflict, as presented in these pages, as it impacts sacred places like the Boundary Waters where I live.

Ultimately books can do no more than begin an awakening to conditions. Being with all our relations, the animals, birds, trees, waters—walking what we know—takes commitment. This vigilance must come from within us each moment. If we were to move daily as Harry suggests we should, as *Total Energy Bodies*, life would become ceremonial. We would engage each other and all other living beings, including rocks and mountains, as brothers and sisters. We would respect and respond to all the diverse medicines, or ways of being-with, rather than standing as aloof as managers, formulators, humans imposing our way as the only way. We would find ourselves happy in sharing all that is given.

Harry springsboards Human Society's intellectual Knowledge, honed over the ages, towards the next step of Super-human development. Intellectual achievement is as necessary to academia as technical ability is to the true artist who wishes to convey her personal "VISION" to paint and canvas, thus uplifting herself and all others who are sensitive to this way of communication. ⌒

Heart Warrior Chosa

A Catechism for the Children of De-Light

Prologue

WHAT IS A CATECHISM?

A catechism is a short manual given in the form of questions and answers as an outline of principles. Principles are what is of first importance. They are how we understand life. These principles are statements which indicate what lies beneath or within all that we say and do. Principles are human beliefs. Principles acted out as beliefs become habitual.

WHO ARE HUMAN BELIEVERS?

Human beings have inhabited planet Earth a very long time, perhaps two million years. Just how long is subject to archeological finds and dating. In northern climates stone-using Acheulian and later Clactorian humans hunted at the edges of the ice during the second Interglacial period (350,000 - 400,000 BCE). More ancient dwelling places in Africa and other southerly climates are probable. Mesolithic humans, using delicately worked tools, were the transition between hunting/food-gathering groups and settled agricultural societies. They populated earth from 25,000 BCE through 3,000 BCE, inhabiting more remote locations even as ancient cities were thriving in warmer locations of India, Africa and the Middle East.

Neolithic stone-using humans developed new social forms based on settled agriculture and lived side by side with people who used bronze and later iron (3,000 - 1,000 BCE). Although bronze-using villages were all over Europe (3,000 - 1,500 BCE) it was the introduction of iron on a mass scale (1,000 - 50 BCE) that allowed the Celts (500 - 50 BCE) to establish a European Empire. Plows, spears and arrowheads, unique art forms, and religious beliefs and practices accompanied wetter, cooler weather during human expansion in this period. Meanwhile, in India, Asia Minor, the Middle East and North Africa, civilizing forces were building megalithic structures and creating iron, copper and bronze tools, including weapons. Archeological evidence strongly suggests that peoples of the Indus Valley moved their cultural and tool-making capabilities throughout Asia Minor, the Middle East and north across Europe from 3,000 BCE onward.

Around 2,500 BCE Aryans, a stone battle-ax people from the North East (Russia), moved across Europe and eventually became the Hittite Kingdom and Mitanni. They spoke languages that are the base for Indo-European languages that unify humans from India throughout Europe. They established cities and brutally crushed early agricultural societies. Fostering notions of business and property they decimated languages and cultural practices that were based in sensitive sensuality and the commons—the more instinctual sharing with all species of land and its bounty.

Human beings, unlike other animals, captured and learned to use FIRE. This fact gave humans the capability to adapt to a variety of living situations. The importance of fire as a basis for expanding consciousness, making humans different from other earthly beings, is primary to understanding the Principles remembered in this Catechism.

Humans also developed, to an ever higher level, the TOOL-USING capabilities seen occasionally in species like otters and ants. Traces of tool-using and fire-building allow us to understand where and how ancient human ancestors lived.

Gradually, humans extended instincts for repetitious noise making into languages. Various forms of pictograph and other symbolic drawings are records of ancient human interactions with their complex world. Everyday life carried on in these languages was not usually recorded until cities formed. However, human beings have always been STORYTELLERS. We engage an experience, then immediately mythologize that experience. Often we recognize our experiences as identical with someone or something previously known. When we express our cognitions of experiences, we storytell. Stories give a sense of order, meaning, safety and security to life lived in every conceivable kind of wild situation.

Shared stories entertain and inform. They are often told around Fires and are sometimes acted out using symbolic, theatrical Tools. Humans absorb stories and use them to shape their realities. These human realities are then often defended as they are practiced. The most revered stories, passed on generation to generation, are those that tell of how a community persisted. These stories reveal a special potency—a resistance to being overpowered by those who would force them, with incompatible stories, to live differently.

Humans consciously sense TIME. Perceptions of earth life processes and the reflections of those processes in the day and night sky give humans the ability to live within conscious awareness of cycle. Stories of cyclic events allow prediction, making humans next to Gods in their ability to project realities onto the world. Human capacities for communication, even in primal stages, passed on knowledge of the elusive keys to life—Fire, Tools, Storytelling and Time—and how humans and their Ways skillfully captured these keys. Hunting, early agriculture, various strategies for shelter and costume, all move in diverse patterns across the planet as the result of the conscious and expressed human acknowledgment of Fire/Tool/Story/Time.

WHERE DO PRINCIPLES COME FROM?

Principles are derived from memory of how we experience life. Principles are not abstract cosmic truths. Principles are always tied to human culture(s), they are collective interpretations of how we are affected by life, generation after generation. Principles stimulate our memory in storytelling. Stories inform us humans through sharply drawn, colorfully focused, images. These images are multidimensional. They are like daily experience. Yet, they contain more. They are visions of how we feel about daily experience. Over the centuries of human interpretation, certain of these images occur again and again. Contained within these recurrent images are teachings, directions for how we are to live. When these teachings are seen and heard, from culture after culture, they reveal similarities. It is these similarities that we call principles.

A Catechism for the Children of De-Light

This Catechism reveals what is common or within all stories. In digging into structural characteristics of all story-telling we probe the underpinnings of human consciousness, our possibilities and limits as a species on this planet.

WHY A 21st CENTURY CATECHISM?

Are humans required to act in principled ways if our species is to survive? All cultures have answered YES to this question. Yet human actions continue to damage and destroy not only our own habitat, but that of thousands of other species. Principled living means to survive with knowledge of universally life-giving actions. Life-Giving actions reflect the basic functioning of all that is, the basic force that is the vast universe. To live Creatively, we must be aware of, i.e. know the story of, how life came to be in all of its variations on earth. Once we know that story we can practice daily life in terms of that story, its power and delicateness.

What are the basic outlines of that story? Earth originated 4.6 billion years ago. The simplest of life forms, classified as Monera (16 phyla—ca. 5,000 described species, potentially 10^8 species) appeared around 4.2 billion years ago. Eubacteria and Archaebacteria have been around at least 3.5 billion years. Protoctists (27 phyla—more than 50,000 species) including algae, diatoms, seaweeds, water molds, chlorophytes, etc. began to flourish over 1 billion years ago and were well established by 700 million years ago. Plants (9 phyla—300,000 species) and Fungi (5 phyla—ca. 100,000 species) were flourishing around 70 million years ago. Animals appeared after this (32 phyla—ca. 10 million species) including everything from mollusks to annelids, echinoderms, arthropods, fishes and vertebrates, including humans. That's our planetary family!

We are differentiated, diverse, but we share common life form building blocks like DNA and mineral-water bodies that are attuned to earth's basic 10 hertz electromagnetic beat. These five life KINDOMS (not "Kingdoms" as conventionally used and implying a hierarchy) are interactively supportive of each other.

A Catechism for the Children of De-Light

There are obviously many more Monera, Bacteria, and Protocists than there are Plants or Animals. Without these basic expressions of life-giving energy, plants and animals cannot exist. This is a late 20th Century Biological version of an ancient understanding of the interrelatedness of all life. Yet, during the era of world wide, corporate-industrial-technology mass culture, humans from all societies have lost touch with (1) the story, and (2), its importance.

Instead of promoting stories that focus on ALL OUR RELATIONS, we most often dignify and encourage stories of conquering, overpowering, and pseudo-reconciliations of relationships within the conquering mode. The DOMINANT HUMAN CULTURE is attuned to "news" of destruction through accident, violence toward each other, and natural climatic catastrophe interpreted as oppressive to industrialized human expression. Our conceit is amazing. Acceptable stories support and further the extractive actions of oil/plastic, consumer driven, international corporate pseudo-principles. What look like statements for living are in reality abusive of life-promoting interactions.

An attitude of human arrogance in relation to all other planetary life makes much of what we collectively do each day dangerous. Statements of impending doom cloud the perceptions of the intelligent, who try to make decisions about our future using information based on stories that repeat what amounts to pieces of wholes, materiality existing without dimension. A 21st Century Catechism is necessary, as humans determine how we can undo the deceptive realities we have created in our own image. Earth is generally a place of worry and fear for most humans at this time. It need not be. By identifying principles within all human storytelling we can retell ourselves into a condition of cosmic De-Light.

HAVE ELECTRONIC MEDIA MADE LIVING BY PRINCIPLE OBSOLETE?

When a person acts without principle s/he is uncivilized. In the late 20th century many people have never been exposed to a catechism. Nor have stories told around the fires of Winter been part of their exposure. Instead we are swept along in flooded rivers of advertising promoted by international corporations (including those of the major world religions) and their respective nation-states. These ads intentionally distort language (image, sign, symbol) to distract humans from our simple earthly/cosmic needs. The power of these ads creates stories where fulfillment is the result of purchasing the latest steel/oil/plastic gadget. Consequently, we live lives adjusting to fad. We expect conformity within a system defined by journalists who are the spokespeople for corporate control, utilizing incredibly powerful electronic media tools. Yet we find little fulfillment, because as soon as we have made conforming adjustments the journalists have shifted the terms of the reality base. Crucial parts of the consumer story change. Without a sense of principled, cosmic purpose, we find ourselves isolated and dysfunctional, unable to act with clear purpose.

Many people, particularly young people, and those who feel outside the dominant culture but totally absorbed by its power, then strike out, using violence, both mechanical and psychic, against a world that seemingly offers no hope. This catechism is written to counteract this condition of cosmic human impotence. Some people have been given catechism. In Christian, Jewish, Islamic and Hindu religious traditions young people are taught principles within stories that are the scriptures, the book, of a particular cosmic viewpoint. Other religions, including those of indigenous peoples, are available to some who honor what has become known as "the Old Way." Scientific-technological training itself has acted as a kind of catechism for intelligent people in the modern era. Awareness of ecological complexity has informed millions of humans that we should act with caring as we use resources. Learning principled living from religions and sciences does help many people live meaningful and creative rather than destructive lives. However, these catechisms are not only anthropocentric, supporting the view that humans are managers of all life, but these principle-style teachings, as orthodoxies, tend to only look at whatever story is being supported rather than the principles themselves which support storytelling.

This catechism looks at what allows stories to work, not just the structural elements of logic and grammar, but the dynamic elements of rhythm and sensibility which are found in all stories and are reflective of cosmic order. For most of us raised in orthodoxies, the catechisms we accepted as children offer little hope as we deal with the complexities of a growing global, total environmental and social hysteria. It is not that some principles within those catechisms are wrong. Rather, it is the fact that those catechisms come from and represent the view of institutions which themselves are consumptive, self-serving, tombs of what may have, at one time, been legitimate attempts to reflect cosmic light. It has become crucial that human decision-making be based on principle rather than greed, because the planetary situation has changed. Demographic projections for humans show another doubling of human populations during the first quarter of the 21st century. The impact on earth processes could be devastating. Or, with principled action, all species could live in quiet, urban/ rural gardens, consciously more integrated with all life than we have since mythic Eden.

Decision-makers need to ask suitable questions to guide development. These questions cannot be formed if basic, universally understood principles are obscured, twisted, shunned. Some principles have been passed through layers and layers of human cultures only to be suppressed by powerful political/religious/economic interests in this and other eras. Often these principles are maintained in non-urban villages all over earth. When spoken, they are the teaching of the wise. These principles are collectively referred to as the OLD WAY. Much of this knowledge never makes it to decision-making chambers where the fate of planet earth is being sealed. In fact, these principles are most often not written. More often they are encoded in ways of talking and being, in stories, in how humans interact with all life around them.

Writing these principles can be seen as a contradiction. The use of technologies based on oil, electricity, extraction of trees and water, additions of chemicals and advertising to make this book available, all violate much of what will be said in the following pages. Ultimately, this attempt at writing these principles will remain an abstraction if what is written is not enacted. Principles may be interesting intellectual constructs, or they may be stimuli for a shifting of human priorities. If future generations of humans and other species are to live with earth, these principles need to be the basis for human management of ourselves and how we interact with all life, now and in the immediate future.

IS THIS A PAGAN CATECHISM?

Part of this book's mission is to establish, as orthodox, beliefs based on principles that are commonly dismissed as pagan. Pagan *paganus* means peasant. Peasants have traditionally been people of the land. Orthodox religions, those who follow dominant beliefs codified as Laws and Covenants, traditionally treat peasants as uneducated. Education is linked closely with training and acceptance of edicts of dominant belief systems, methods, classifications. Education is bestowed on selected members of elite, politically powerful humans who see themselves as decision-makers and guardians of life on earth.

Throughout human urban history various culturally approved priests, including those of religious, scientific, and metaphysical persuasions, have created books and institutions to insure perpetuation of their doctrines. In effect, these elites have enshrined their STORIES. In modern times a bourgeoisie or economic middle class has been encouraged to partake of dominant forms of elite education. Scientific methodologies have made it seem that truth is not a function of belief, that human knowledge as taught by dominant culture institutions is not entwined with economic and social world power. Meanwhile, for thousands of years, elites of urban cultures, posing as civilizing forces, have systematically suppressed human knowledge passed on by those who continue close ties with the land, the cosmos, and all life giving processes. This repression has led to abnormal patterns of human behavior, particularly as urban human centers have sprawled over the landscape.

This catechism looks from within restrained pagan knowledge, informed by immediate worldly contact and tradition passed through STORY, through signs and symbols shared by all stories, to find cornerstones that are within all beliefs, principles that are within all human determinations. The principles elucidated in this catechism are primary. They are primal, in the sense that all humans, from hunter/gathers through space age voyagers, utilize these principles as we storytell.

In Western culture the word pagan describes any person whose religious beliefs are neither Christian, Moslem or Jewish. This would then mean that during the Judeo-Christian era the majority of the people on the planet are pagan. Pagan has never implied non-believer: pagans have never been understood as agnostic or atheistic. Rather, pagan is a distinctly derogatory term aimed at peoples who are usually termed idol worshippers by orthodoxies who themselves revere idols, but who have ruthlessly dominated human destiny, particularly since 1139 CE, after the Lateran Council, which was the beginning of the Inquisition.

The term heathen is used synonymously with pagan to describe those who are not converts to Christianity, Islam or Judaism. Much of the attitude of non-tolerance implied in the use of words like heathen or pagan stems from the Old Testament word Gentile. Gentile originally referred to the non-Jew who practiced what were defined as polytheistic religions. Polytheistic religious practices were usually more oriented to a specific place's agricultural practices. In fact a case can be made that the historic people of the Old Testament were themselves land based tribes. But they saw themselves as special after a particular incident. They were 'chosen,' and through sacred covenant with God (Yahweh or Jehovah, the Hebrew Tetragrammaton JHVH or JHWH or YHVH or YHWH), were given Laws, making all manifestations of religious practice, which differed from theirs, invalid. Symbols and signs used by other religious languages were said to be idolatrous. Thus a stigma was placed on other cultures.

Jewish tribes and their priest class were not the only practitioners of such intolerance. Most tribal peoples during the solar/patriarchal Age of Aries (1940 BCE- 220 CE) saw themselves as unique and receptors of Divine Laws. Many had a notion of direct favor with s/he who created.

Religions based on oral transmissions coded on clay tablets, from Greece and Phoenicia throughout the Middle East and Asia Minor and into India and China, reflected the fiery male power of the Ram on polarity with Libran scales of justice. Sheepherding peoples, watching the fierceness and "I' ness" of the individual fathering Ram could well have interpreted the creator of all life as such a creature. "Thou shalt have no other before me" is visible in pasture behavior. One creator God above and outside all other gods, in special covenant/law relationship with a chosen people, was the basis of monotheism. Urban temple dwellers interpreted Divine Law to mean driving out all who did not obey.

The old gods of the Taurus Age (4100 BCE- 1940 BCE), symbolized by the all-giving Bull/Buffalo/Ox on polarity with the Serpent/Dragon, were considered wrong or evil—at best only an ancient, outmoded story. This is a crucial turning point in earth history and human storytelling/knowledge/education. As alphabets were formed and writing replaced oral transmission, making temple sites sacred holding places of Divine Laws, intolerance turned to conquering. Bronze and iron swords, chariots and horses were signs of defense of each people's sacred rights.

During the Taurus Age and before, all the way back to the beginning of humans living on a planet that went from periodic Ice Ages (250,000 years typical duration) to warmer periods that were often of shorter duration, earth was understood as a commons. All living creatures, including rocks, the smallest insects, fish, plants and animals were recognized as necessary for each others existence. All were seen as devouring, but all knew their place as those who would be devoured. EARTH, WATER, AIR AND FIRE created a planetary home for us all. No one owned, no one managed, no one was the custodian of destiny. Serpentine water/ fire energies were allowed to do their creative tasks, instinctively, sensually, commonly, without imposed human restriction.

Unfortunately, during the Pisces Age (220 CE - 2380 CE) on polarity with Virgo, humans have rigorously enforced the rules of Divine Law written in sacred books, based on the tribal intolerance of the previous Aries Age cultures. In typical Piscian character, while Law prevails, sensitive earth knowledge becomes foggy, hazy. Humans forget how to relate in an immediate sense with basic life giving processes, redefining knowledge of the commons in terms of individual psychology, pretending then that ultimate power resides within the individual as that particular individual acts in terms of the accepted dominant culture Laws. This stance has allowed the privatization of the commons, even down to the corporate.

PART I
PRINCIPLES OF CONTEXT

"When consciousness (cit) enters substance (sat)
delight (ananda) appears."
— Alain Daielou —

"Energy is Eternal Delight."
— William Blake —

"$E = M C^2$"
— Albert Einstein —

"On Earth, all entities formed within the 10-hertz
discharge—and all of their descendents—would
resonate at the same frequency or show extreme
sensitivity to it."
— John Becker M.D. —

A Catechism for the Children of De-Light

HOW LARGE IS YOUR WORLD?

Every person's story is based in a cosmology. Even the most basic memory/thought of an action entails all that is and can be known, because we use forms of language, sign, symbol, archetype, formulae, pattern when we think. We communicate with ourselves and others with assumptions about the nature of reality that shape, but are often not revealed as, the basis from which our story operates. Cosmological stories are themselves of such grand scope that they are passed along as myth or legend. They are the basis of whole cultures and religions. Yet, everything we know about ourselves, individually and collectively, places us in ever larger contexts. When we tell of an experience, how we speak entails and conveys how we see ourselves in the universe.

As infants we are in constant relationship with other/Mother. We sense dependence in all ways. She is All, except for our own sense of being. She is our cosmos until we gradually become aware of the planetary world, the sky, the vast depths of nightly heavens. In that awareness we sense a grand scale interdependence, not unlike that which we feel with mother. In pagan cultures, Cosmic Mother, Earthly Mother and human mother are dimensional reflections of each other. Even the more mystic versions of monotheistic religions hold creation in motherly context.

We learn that we, and other animals, come from mothers. We learn that many plants come from seeds. Watching insects and simpler life forms we see that individuals are born of other individuals. So it is a natural, child's curiosity to wonder where the planet comes from, where the sun comes from, where stars and the whole universe come from.

Our stories generally imitate one of two cosmological contexts passed generation to generation. The pagan cosmos is ALL THAT IS. The monotheistic/orthodoxies' cosmos is *a creation of, an emanation of,* the unnameable, the infinite. These are two very different awarenesses. In the pagan context, total-moment-experiences in all their harmony, beauty, cruelty, dissonance, are illuminations of ALL THAT IS, including that which is beyond human understanding. In the monotheistic view our human experience is established or confined within parameters set by the ONE yet outside of any direct experience that reflects the creative ordering. Human experiences are judged in terms of Laws, rules, appeals to that ONE.

Pagan cosmological conceptions entail galactic whirls as larger forms of coiled serpents, each unfolding like the process of becoming shared by all life forms. Breathing by a human or a whale is the same action as the expansion or contraction of the universe itself. What happens in our daily lives is what happens everywhere, forever.

Monotheistic cosmology entails hierarchy. The upper world, or place of the Creator/Nourisher/Divine Mind, can only be approached through prayers, worship, mediation. Aspects of creation can be seen in the material world, daily affairs and human history. But Ein Sof (unknowable Infinity) is not the Sefirot (ten emanations) which are the basis of human knowledge of the unspeakable/G d.

The language of pagan attunement with life is often confused with monotheistic viewpoints. This is particularly true with conceptions from Solar cultures. Because our Sun is venerated as a male or female source necessary for life, and because this honor usually involves a priestly patriarchy, assumptions of interchangeability between Sun and the monotheistic ONE, the unspeakable Creator, are made. Mithraic, Celtic, Germanic pagan traditions are infused into Christianity with this confusion. In America indigenous natives continue to struggle with this confusion. Medicine people remind "you can't have it both ways." This means that celebration of our oneness with All and worship of the One are very different practices. How we walk among all creatures of life is very different based on which of these traditions we accept as our context for reality. How we, individually and collectively, make decisions, either as members of cosmic commons or as elected human elite, determines our destiny.

A Catechism for the Children of De-Light

WHOSE STORY ARE YOU TELLING?

50,000 to 500,000 years of storytelling means that every time we speak our fresh experience we do so in terms of all kinds of meanings, senses of ordering, theories, worries, dreams, and cultural myths. Because we speak as human beings the contexts of our remembrances of 'what just happened' are encoded in ancestral linguistic environments.

In our time it is most likely that our stories will reflect the cosmological underpinnings of the greatest economic/military empire ever assembled on Earth, the American market-economy hegemony. The cosmology that drives this Empire is Judeo-Christian. An anthropomorphized, male Creator ordered and started the universe billions of years ago according to their story. Modern science plays into this part of the story. This creator created (in an image of himself) a man who subsequently separated off a part of himself into a sexual opposite, woman. This happened in a mythical place and past. That same creator evidently took time off, for it wasn't until about 5,000 years ago that He again spoke and gave Laws to his chosen tribe of people. And it was only 2,000 years ago that He decided to show humans the path to salvation through institutions related to his Son. This reiterated monotheistic story allows a community, and the officials appointed by that community, to claim that because they are chosen they have power to dominate. Their might is Divinely Right. Expansionist dominion over 'all' is their elected destiny. Christianity, Judaism, Islam, are theistic practitioners of this story. Marxism is an atheistic version of the same cosmology.

A conscious listener can immediately tell if the dominant culture's version of theism underlies what they hear in the stories of various people as they relate their experiences. Most people's contexts are rather narrow, surface, and betray an acceptance of privileged consumption. As the American Empire has spread throughout poorer, overexploited countries, people who claim to come from non-monotheistic pagan perspectives speak their experiences with the symbols, signs, meanings of the cultural practices that have conquered them. We live more and more each day in a world where the "information highway" appears one of diversity, but actually betrays contextual confusion. This is especially true as we try to deal with (manage) the environmental mess that a modern, consumptive, empire has brought.

In the context of the dominant cosmic paradigm the world is split between that which is of the Creator/Caretaker/Nourisher/Judge, and that which is of the body, material, tangible, observable. The connections between the world of the Spirit and the rest of reality are often couched in terms of Mind, Consciousness, Soul. It is important to listen in all stories from this perspective for the anthropomorphic/humanized version of cosmic realities. When terms like All or Unity or One are used from this perspective, within the story which follows you will find that these terms reflect human reference. Their contextual meanings are derived from supposing the universe to be a reflection of human-like Will/Intention/Attention.

From a pagan perspective, whatever is Infinite, unspeakable, beyond our knowledge, is life within all beings, animate and inanimate. There is no Creator out there, somewhere, hidden in space. Creation is constant, continual, happening within each breath, each moment. There was not some distant act that began a chain reaction of cause and effect that has ended in our superior species. Rather a continual, ever present, infinite sea of energy unfolds in a myriad of predictable and unpredictable forms, materializations, dimensional realities, only a few of which manifest moment to moment through humanity's six senses. The pagan world is one of appearances and disappearances, of continual motion, change, of openings into this reality only to transfigure, metamorphose, transmute, convert into yet another disclosure. Nothing is fixed. Dynamic creation is set within tension, paradox, tendency, focus and dissolve, within infinite diversity.

Ancient languages work to communicate the continually activating nature of the pagan realities. It is more difficult to communicate the experiences of the infinitely 'knowable,' the ineffable, within the grammar of Indo-European-style language forms. We must be very careful when attempting to convey pagan awe, mystery, understanding, in languages usually used to speak dominant culture themes. An example: A compassionate Creator nourishes and cares for all creatures, therefore giving to humans the Law 'thou shalt not kill,' or do not uproot or kill unless it is necessary. Pagan, peasant awareness is that killing to eat is the process of continual creation. While both stories may reflect anti-violence in their telling, the interactive attitudes/intentions regarding killing/death are, however, very different. The dominant culture's morality allows it to design and direct necessity. Killing/death is the antithesis/obstacle to be overpowered in the quest for human permanence. The pagan attitude assumes that killing is a process that will also effect whatever humans design or direct. The revelation of that process may be sudden, as in an earthquake or hurricane, or it may be geological in time scale, e.g. microbes and winds teaming up over centuries to make a human monument into a heap of sand.

Cosmic contexts within human stories expose the stakes: what the believer/teller risks to gain reward. Acceptance of dominant contexts allows relaxation, conceit, complacence. Monotheistic hierarchy as a cosmic context for our stories means we are willing to risk living within totalitarian empire so that we can languish in consumption. This is the humanistic fallacy, that we can act as remote Creators, Gods, Fixers, making an expressionist painting of all that was created for our fancy.

Living stories rooted in cosmic contexts which are pagan, polytheistic, of the commons, means we are willing to risk being outsiders, living obscure, poor, wretched existences as viewed by dominant culture standards. By pagan standards we find our De-Light, our joy, our ever unfolding awakening to earth-cosmic harmony by becoming All That Is, by recognition of our Total Energy-bodies interacting in reflective continual creation. For us even the simplest movements of an ant within our contextual moment are cause for celebration of galactic exposure.

IS (WAS) THERE A BEGINNING?

In this physical world of bodies, things, stuff, everything appears to come from something else, or is the result of mergings. Earth and Sun had their beginnings. No one knows for sure precisely when or how. But in the age of scientific perception we observe the births of stars, planets, asteroids with powerful telescopes, on Earth or within space probes. We also observe novas or apparent deaths of heavenly bodies. Still, the question haunts us, was there a beginning to all these stars, planetary systems, the galaxies in which they move? Was there a time without time, space without space?

Many physicists speak in a metaphor about space/time having a beginning in a bang, an incredible explosion. Of what? Compressed gasses, all of which could be squeezed tightly in a human hand. Aren't gases a form of physical reality, which is dependent upon space/time? What came before gases? Nothing? Emptiness? According to their metaphor all began from a tiny massing. All since has been and continues to be expansion. Into what? Can we really conceive of emptiness?

The Kabbala of Judaism and Buddhism conceive a mystic merging with the Infinite Mystery of Nothingness as a goal. Ein Sof is pure ether. We may merge with it, but we will never know of it. From these theistic viewpoints we are limited humans. Beyond us is a vastness which is impenetrable. Attitudes of prayer or meditation can receive emanations from that unknown, and those emanations are the roots of human wisdom.

For monotheists the causal Creation question, given a remote Creator, is "was there a first emanation?" For pagans the question is one of moments in creative unfoldment. In a historic sense a 'bang' might seem important. But a spoken word, a galactic spark, any cosmic scale event could be seen as a beginning. More importantly, every moment of events is a continual beginning, continual conception. History, understood as sacred for monotheists, may be a trick of human memory, as understood by pagans. Simultaneous bangs beginning creations may be happening all round us throughout our conception of space/time.

In the monotheistic Creation stories, God gets to feel delight then withdraws into a vacuum, forming an amorphous mass surrounded by Light. Out of this mass emanations of four worlds came: emanation, creation, formation, actualization. In pagan stories there is no One male who withdraws. There are ever present Gods and Goddesses, characters who describe Total Energy-Body interactions, non-materialized but continually manifesting. These non-materialized characters are greater than humanity in an archetypal sense: They are the tendencies toward/from which all life patterns its interactions. They embody all that happens in the commons.

Shiva/Zeus/Dionysus/Kokopelli are all ictophallic signs (idols) of life giving/producing, ejaculating processes. Shakti, Parvati, Athena, Anu, Macha, mother goddesses through which manifestation becomes, are but a few of the characters who carry birthing functions in stories of all cultures. What bangs in human understanding is the tension between these characters/forces. Their merging is necessary for continual creation to happen. But they are up front anthropomorphized forms of forces which are universal. These forces are best described as polarities in a male/female dance. Electromagnetic, molecular pulsations, in a moment of cosmic lightning/fire bring about a beginning/being as the result of their unifying dance. Shiva/Shakti dances creation's unfoldment. We enact that ceremony with each breath, each interactive movement in material or manifested reality.

All creatures from microorganisms to fungi to plants to animals share, sense, emanate this life-giving energy. Rocks, gases, all kinds of wave energies, including light, move through myriad of dimensional realities—coming into being, only to fade away as they become some other manifestation. Constant, creative permeation is this infinite, ever-ongoing, impregnating activity. Simultaneous bangs, continual beginnings, that is the expansiveness of all creation.

HOW CAN WE SENSE THIS ALL-PERVASIVE ACTIVATING ENERGY?

Sacred places are where electromagnetic, life-giving, pulsating energies are concentrated. These places are themselves receiver/transmitter centers on Earth. The most pervasive place in pagan stories is the mountain. Mount Maru, probably located in our time in the Himalayan range in Tibet, is the mythic mountain at the center of cosmic touch with Earth. All over Earth, in all cultures, sacred mountains, particularly those which have the classic four-sided, pyramidal shape, are held as special places for awakening of cosmic energies within humans. The sacred, four-sided mountain awareness was carried by our ancestors about 6,000 BCE down the great river(s) of India out across the oceans and was the "base" which inspired the form of pyramids throughout Asia Minor, the Middle East, and the Americas. The Sun Priests (and Priestesses) receive and transmit from the top of this sacred form/place. Questers, initiates, seekers, climb this proverbial mountain, following the spiral path of the galactic whirl/coiled serpent.

The human body is itself a receiver/transmitter of magnificent potential when awakened. All pagan cultures have located seven centers/sacred places where cosmic connective energies can focus and whirl. In all cultures, sitting in the crossed-leg yoga pose sets the human body in the sacred mountain form. In that pose, breath is concentrated, sharpened; each breath brings in the galactic-whirling-cosmic-mother-birthing energies. They are brought into the place of the first chakra, the coccyx, located at the base of the spine, the base of the mountain. Here lies the kundalini energy of awakening, coiled as a serpent, asleep. Its awakening and gradual uncoiling is the galactic whirl invigorating our receptive/transmitter Total Energy-bodies. In awakening, energy centers associated with the genitals, the solar plexus, the heart, throat/mouth, third eye, and crown or top of the head are breathed and stretched into pulsating action. The Total Energy-Body, the eighth place of unfoldment, merged with the totality of the pulsating universe, is now magnetically linked with its Earthly position. It is capable of drawing in and transmitting outward vibratory qualities associated with dimensions outside those recognized by five human senses. The sixth sense, intentionally activated, is cosmic/energy/fire.

There are places in the Earth's magnetosphere that are energetically hot. These apparently are linked with the planetary inner molten liquid, its continual digestion of and spewing forth of giant earth plates, some of that energy coming closer to the earth places we know. Many of these places have been known for thousands of years. Throughout all cultures we find that either outdoor ritual materials or temples and cathedrals are located on these places, sometimes known as crossing points of leylines, magnetic pathways that are within Earth and its atmosphere.

In our noisy world you can feel a different energy around these places. If you are an initiate, practicing the daily activation of galactic energy uncoiled, being a receiver/transmitter, recognizing yourself and all life as resonate within a resonate universe, these places allow for a greater attunement, a heightening of your body's resistors so that more intense forms of cosmic energy can be handled by your Total Energy-Body.

Go to one of these places, hopefully one that will allow you to be totally alone, away from all humans, as quiet as you can be given the industrial world's background noise. Sit. Become the mountain. Close your eyes and focus on breathing the whole galaxy into you. Allow the serpent to uncoil, activating all your energy centers. As the Total Energy-body activates you will feel the De-Light of continual creation.

Some of the most sacred places on Earth are caves, entries into the energy fields of the Earthly Mother. She is granddaughter of the cosmic whirl—the Galactic Grandmother. When we sit in classic yoga/cross-legged position that forms the pyramidal mountain with our Energy-body potential, we are within the mountain. Many stories are of the uncoiling of the serpentine/cosmic fire energy within the mountain, of our human initiations being equivalent to volcanic energies. The inner cave (looks within), is where we see/feel/sense cosmic fire energy most intensely. So these places are linked with death of the physical body, with burial, and with rebirth in a different Total Energy-body form. Caves tunneled into rocks all over earth have always been sacred human places. Underground ritual/teaching structures such as Kivas in the American Southwest and similar structures throughout the Middle East and Far East attest to the importance of proper place in Total Energy-body living. Inner caves within Earth/bodies reflect the vast CAVE universe.

Many inner places are linked with water, either as a place where water bubbles from within Earth herself, or as a holding place for water cycled through air, returned to earth as rain. Water is the medium through which cosmic vibrating energies work with earthly bodies, physical forms. We are crystalline/mineral, yes; but we are mostly bodies of water. Activating kundalini is bringing fire to water, as in heating water, thus activating the molecular structure.

The coiled Serpent/fire Dragon reflects the emanating galactic whirl(s) that provide life. Clay or woven pottery was/is a daily reminder of the receptive vessel holding water. In Celtic culture the Grail holds this significance. It is interesting to remember that monotheistic cultures, Christian and Moslem, perpetuate stories of dragon slaying as the highest role for human/warrior/heroes defending and conquering, these actions backed by divine right. Places where this energy is/was enacted have been trampled by the dominant cultures of the last two thousand years. Which is why so much of pagan culture is carried out in secret.

IS THERE EMPTINESS, NOTHINGNESS?

Monotheistic cultures conceive of an Infinite, a boundlessness which is concealed from all creatures. This great expanse of prelife cannot be understood, yet Judaism, mystic Christianity and Buddhism call this nothingness the place of becoming. Wisdom is said to come from nothingness, as are manifesting emanations.

A Catechism for the Children of De-Light

From a pagan perspective even this nothingness is not separate from ever-creating energies. Only our inability to open ourselves to continual creating makes emptiness seem non-fulfilling. All is filled with De-Light (ful) activity. De-Light—effervescent and ever-creating—moves around rigidified, blocked, compacted and entropy-inducing activity. Energies that suck inward, operate defensively, eventually consume themselves, and also often consume unaware, unawakened, uninitiated Total Energy-bodies around them. What appears dark, negative, blocked, collapsing into and through entropy, becomes available for merging with creating energies in other moments.

IS DE-LIGHT SACRED?

Where humans direct our *attention* is all-important. Attention, that quality of focusing all our six senses, is a creating activity. What we pay attention to sets the context of our moment-to-moment human world. Intention, or transmitting into the world, influences how momentary manifestations unfold. Total Energy-body projections affect even the seemingly simplest of life forms. All other species 'read' humans in this way; their attention energies sensing our intentions for shaping shared realities. Total Energy-body projections are non-local. They are not space/time dependent. In pagan cultures, initiates can communicate, effect healing, change the course of events far away, across the world, by focusing Total Energy-body energies in an intended pattern. Humans are very powerful in this way. And, non-initiates bring much destruction to the world by focusing without knowledge of what they are doing, without regard for the welfare of ALL, with incredible greed. Attempted healings with bad intentions or restricting or twisted attitudes can hurt what we're trying to help. Even initiated people can project negative influences.

If we pay attention to fears, let them control our Total Energy-body, we project defenses. If we do this continually, moment to moment, De-Light glances off these energy de-fences. We can become islands of self-consumptive energies.

However, if we pay attention to the vast sea of De-Light activating creation permeating all facets of every being, place, interactive relationship, there is an awe at how vast this presence is, continually. This feeling of reverential awe makes our experience of De-Light sacred. That sense of sacredness can happen anytime, anyplace, in any dimension of reality, including what we call dreams. The key to experiencing the joy of De-Lightful living is to be continually aware of, awakened to, the cosmic context within each experiential moment. Pay attention! Remember, your intentions are your potency, your power. For that power to feel De-Lightful it must be transmitted from you creatively, infusing the world of All-else with further De-Light. All actions done in this way are sacred, holy, emulations of the all-pervading creative becoming.

WOULD DE-LIGHT HAPPEN WITHOUT HUMANS?

Humans as two legged, upright, conscious, Total Energy-body projectors/transmitters share De-Light, pure joy, with other species. That is why pagans have such affinity with birds, animals, trees, all plants, all the creatures of the waters. When we are attuned we communicate in a totally open way, without distraction or interference. Without humans around, this kind of communication goes on continually. All beings, animate and so called inanimate, project their Total Energy-bodies. The world of microscopic life, insects, fungi, plants, animals, rocks, winds, all communicate, inform, teach, give messages. Without that activity, life would not be. De-Light emanates from every creating aspect, forever.

IS IT POSSIBLE FOR DE-LIGHT TO CEASE TO BE?

The focus of our attention and our attitude can give us Total Energy-body sensations of sadness, loneliness, depression. How we focus our resonance can be negative. We can kill creative resilience. Energy blockages for whatever reason are the essence of sickness. Eventually their rigidity self-destructs to become creating activity again, simply going in a direction away from that which it was. Or, we can effectively change that resonance, bring about healing. Sometimes this takes another being with a De-Lightfilled attitude, a shaman. Her/his intention can overpower a sickened Energy-body, help it absorb its sickness, recycle it into well being.

De-Light is eternal, never ending, the central process that makes all dimensions happen. Our recognition of De-Light as ongoing creation is the essential for appreciating the vast possibilities within infinitely-present-moment life.

CAN DE-LIGHT BE NAMED?

"He who knows does not speak.
He who speaks does not know."
— Lao Tzu —

The limits of human understanding are reached as soon as we attempt to use words or signs or symbols. Any language is based in belief reflecting a cosmic context. When we codify we step outside the De-Light process. At best we express a moment which already passed. Hebrew, Greek, Siouan, Arabic, Sanskrit, or English each function with an internal logic and a set of contextual meanings. We try to record the processes, experiences, revelations we participate in. But being a Total Energy-body within De-Light activation is not speaking, writing or drawing about it. It may be dancing or enacting it, two forms of ritual celebration which, accompanied by rhythmic music, can enhance focus and actually help initiate De-light activation.

All languages are religious in the sense that each faces the impossibility of communicating what their primary subject is. What is that subject? Some say *the uniting of what is separated*. Which is to say that whenever we think, speak, write, attempt any kind of transmission of knowledge or understanding we are enacting connectives, activating the cosmos. In monotheistic religions where divine laws are in words, where divine scriptures accompany these laws, the word itself can be divine. Creation itself is a result of the Creator speaking. In pagan cultures, especially those which are solar, and probably have a common root in Shivism of 6,000 BCE India, attention to words is part of what an initiate learns. Hunbatz Men, the great contemporary teacher of the Mayan people, in his book *Secrets of Mayan Science and Religion*, shows what is in words like ***kundalini, k'ultanlini, k,ulthanlini,*** not only linking solar-serpentine cultures from different world places, but when inverted, as we are taught to do, unveiling common cosmic understandings. Pagan initiates are often taught to pay attention to individual letter sounds within words, for they convey cosmic context. We are also taught to invert words and phrases as another process of awakening. G is a letter sound found all over the planet and signifying sacred beginnings, the cosmic spiral/galactic whirl. O is associated with awakened consciousness. D or T (depending upon language) indicates the processes of emanation, how resonance is recognized/received.

Orthodox Judaic/Christian/Islamic practitioners are very careful in voicing what they consider the unspeakable, the Infinite, Unknowable, Creator. When written, the name G d is often written without a letter. When spoken, G O to the D is not used with familiarity. You do not say G_d in the same way you say George or Rachel. Naming changes cosmic context into character. The placement of a reserved name on that which is at the center of a religious faith is not unique to these accepted orthodoxies. The name Tirawa in Siouan languages is similar to God, Allah, Yahweh in invocation. Woden and other Celt/Germanic Gods may have had similar status in solar cultures.

The reserved nature of a named Creator implies an attitude of worship of One who is outside His/Her creations. Naming entails an object for what is named, and in this case, an object which is understood to have primary human qualities. The call or prayer is directed to this name. Intercession is requested, or thanks for existing conditions is offered. As soon as this reserved name is used, all the language baggage associated with that name is operative: theologies, liturgies, rituals, required attitudes and intentions for successful communion.

In orthodox religions, as well as in pagan practices which name deities, an attitude of reverence accompanies the mention of that name. But reverence in worship is different from reverence in celebration. Celebration is inclusive. Deities, Gods and Goddesses of pagan traditions are usually understood as names for processes, projections of Total Energy-bodies which each of us does or is capable of doing/being. The interactions of these Gods and Goddesses (central characters) are an expression of the state of tension, which is the principle of creation and the nature of all divine being. When we attune our Total Energy-bodies with these divine interactions we feel the ecstasy; the freeing of inhibitions which is mystical attunement. We sense De-Light. We do not name it. De-Light is not a deity.

De-Light identifies a human feeling with an all pervasive creating energy. For this reason De-Light carries the God correspondence for many 'mystic' and/or heretical traditions even within the orthodoxies. This confusion is central to much misunderstanding and many attempts to fuse pagan experience with orthodox dogma. Children of De-Light do not deify. They therefore have no need to codify. Stories of De-Light(ful) experience are passed generation to generation. Yet these do not constitute a religion. They are intended as teachings that show how De-Light has manifested through all kinds of life-forms on Earth and in other dimensions. The point of these teaching stories and characters is to provide adequate images for enhancing mystery, the presence of ever-creating Beauty in the material world and other dimensions. In pagan cultures many traditional stories are also known as "personal." Stories reveal our unfoldment, the processes of how we become ever more total, our explosion/bang/movement outward, merging with mystery as we awaken to ever deeper/wider dimensional meanings/realities. Our relationships to the characters in these stories are very important for our personal sense of ordering and change.

A Catechism for the Children of De-Light

Gods and Goddesses who are part of our childhood awareness grow as we grow, their adventures and overpowering of obstacles reflecting for us our spiral unwinding of tension. It is not important that we figure out our personal life in a rational/psychologically consistent manner. Rather, the depths of our personhood should become manifest to us through the processes of story.

Naming Gods/Goddesses often has to do with place. These primary characters in life drama have experiences of their own or experiences in conjunction with humans in a locality. Humans in hunter/gatherer and agricultural societies sense the presence of beings living in dimensions that interact with Earth conditions but are not materially manifested, except through alliance with human, animal or other species' activity. Teaching stories in pagan cultures are usually specific to an area that is familiar to the people who are hearing the story. Gods/Goddesses may act very similarly in the stories of different peoples, but the locality of the story will be significantly different, and often there are slight differences in how the name of that God/Goddess is said. Yet, when we hear these stories we see the similarities.

The context of pagan stories usually includes other sets of characters whose names are spoken with reverence, but who are not specifically Gods/Goddesses. In Celtic and indigenous American Indian cultures, Ancestors (those who have gone before) are central figures in ceremonies, stories, awareness. Their presence is requested. They are the source of knowledge about how to live within this materialized dimension. These Ancestors may be thousands of years old, but in the dimensional realities that are outside of the limits of space/time their presence is ageless. Their wisdom cuts across barriers of current fad. Total Energy-body interaction with Ancestors is a constant source of comfort and De-Light. They offer advice, guidance and perception from outside our human perspective. Usually they are seen/heard as heads. The traditions of severed heads, talking heads in Celtic, American Indian, and Oriental story-teachings tell of our relationships with Ancestors.

A Catechism for the Children of De-Light

Other names that are sometimes thought to convey Godlike characteristics exist in many cultures that maintain a close link with Animals. All Animals are potential teachers; some hold places in cultural stories as creators. Coyote, Raven, Snake, create through shapeshifting—the ability to assume a shape other than their usual form. Stag, Buffalo/Bull, Eagle and Hawk all have powers which rival those of Ancestors and God/Goddesses. Sometimes names for dimensional creatures are interrelated, as in the Feathered Serpent of the Yucatan, Quetzalcoatl or Kukulcan, or Ganesha the elephant-headed God of India. Christian missionaries and soldiers coming into a rich, multi-dimensional culture like that of the Mayan/Celt/ Shivite (in fact most human cultures on this world) perceive, as Gods, Animals, Ancestors and human activity mix in a creative dance, not the celebration—the immense joys of awakened living—but idolatry. Monotheists miss out on the immediacy of continual creation, having accepted the postulation of some remote beginning with a single Godhead as the source for material reality. Attempts by Monotheists to crush pagan culture are always doomed to failure, precisely because so much of the culture operates outside three-dimensional human conceptions. Continuity is maintained by personages within cultural tradition who are not necessarily of flesh and blood.

DOES NAMING A CREATOR CARRY OTHER IMPLICATIONS?

The invocation of the name GOD, in whatever language, not only has the character of being special or set-aside within a cultural understanding, it means greater than, ruler, Supreme. God is the highest power, the final authority, the dominant being. In using the name God we have set up a hierarchical relationship, linguistically speaking, and we are immediately thrust in the realm of political language and worship. The dominant orthodoxies have included in their naming of the deity an acceptable ordering for human life in the universe. Christianity, Islam and Judaism are all religions of Law. The relationship between God the Supreme

Being and the person or community invoking the name is one of covenant. A solemn pledge or agreement, a compact filled with promise and obedience, is made when the name is spoken. Gods/ Goddesses, Ancestors, Animals invoked in pagan cultures do not function in the same legal relationship. They are instead energies of a more intense dimensional nature, resonances that are faster than background Earth and regular human/animal/plant resonances.

In the dominant culture the named God in relationship with a religious community becomes associated with what is legal or right. It is easily assumed that a covenant resulting in different sets of rules implies a variant God. The Supreme Ruler of the universe has correspondences, and thus shares traits, with human Kings, Queens, Fathers or Mothers. Among the orthodoxies the notion of God the Father, the Supreme Ruler, the Supreme Being is chosen as the model of organization implied in the name God. All other conceptions are deemed wrong, and the term 'pagan' applied to them.

Confusions result when pagan cultures speak of the Cosmic Mother or the Solar God/Sun/Father, meaning the energies emanating from the Milky Way and the Eye, or the perceiving center of that emanation associated with a Central Sun. The natural ordering resulting from galactic swirls is not necessarily consistent with rules given to a chosen community by a Law Giver. Goddesses like Tlachtga, Thunderbolt-Wisdom Woman of the Irish Celtic tradition, kindler of FIRE(s), and associated with a black hill with meteoric origins, Parvati-She Of The Mountain in India, and Al-Uzza the pre-Islamic Goddess whose black stone is *Kaaba* at Mecca, are of the Cosmic Wheel. Gods and Goddesses are elements of the sense of place, cyclic timing, shared energies that make all life one. It is very important to distinguish between Creator God(s) who are causes of a creation and those Gods who are continually creating all of the dimensions, which are seen and unseen aspects of the realities we understand. In our time of ecological disaster there are those who would retranslate the notion of dominion over all that resides in the Hebrew Old Testament, trying to make the dominant culture's destruction of Earth an accident of translation. The dogma of Law-giving God(s) is no mishap of language usage. It is a very definite, human-oriented view of how life is to be lived on Earth. That conception allows for consumption at endangering levels. The pagan, peasant, primitive understanding of how interactive cosmic creation works does not condone or stimulate dominating, devouring, destruction.

The conception of God as Supreme Law Giver means that those humans who receive those Laws act in accord with the deity. They are chosen. The acknowledged orthodoxies have all generated systems of legal codes, sacred and secular, which because they embody the divine, allow for no one to live outside these Laws. Once a system of divine Laws is invoked, the whole apparatus of 'civilization' sets limits, imposed by force if necessary. Limit-setting of this kind inflicts energy blockages, disrupting the creative activation of De-Light. Human thought forms, i.e. rational, logical, patterns imposed on action are barriers to sensing the creative energies that continually make each moment new. Retreats away from the power of these civilizing forces allow a few humans to stay in touch with De-Light. These few tell the stories of De-Light(ful) experiences so that others, over the generations, are reminded that the life force flowers despite imposed, authoritarian, legal rigidities.

'Civilization,' as most people know it, rewards those who develop their lives within the Law. Institutions are formed to preserve that divine legal system, to pass it through narrowly-conceived "education," generation after generation. Ideas, including alternate cosmologies, that do not support the conceptual structure of "civilized" institutions are banned, punished, made unacceptable by branding with words like romantic, communistic, primitive, peasant, or pagan. Rewards for remaining within the legal/divine/even scientific-rational system are comfort and success measured in material goods. Market economies depend for their authority on forcing agreement on the naming of the accepted God, giver of Law, as a divine system within which rules must be obeyed. In the late 21st Century the word democracy has been used (misused) as an economic code word indicating adherence to economic manifestations of the monotheistic civilizing force backed by divine-given sanction. In the name of democracy and freedom, 'chosen' humans are unifying the planet to rid it of pagan influence.

Children who sense De-Light often go away from the centers of Law, the Holy Cities. We go deep into forests or on far mountains. We try to do this for long periods of time, to remove ourselves from the human (God) bombardment of what seems to us legal lies perpetrated by the dominant culture. You must get away from the noise, away from dammed up streams, away from speeding machines, to again sense the gentle ease of continuous creation. Those of us who do, touch De-Light(ful) flowing energy life in two worlds. We know and sense cosmic joyfulness. At the same time we know and sense the weight of imposed Law manifesting as the conquering of all life by humans. We function as cosmic half-breeds, living in two distinctly separate worlds. It is painful to witness the destructive resistance to De-Light, which is now dominant and overpowers the beauty of Earth.

DOES NAMING GOD IMPLY MORE THAN LAW?

The naming of God does not simply imply Ruler and Law. In the Old Testament the most popular name for God is Elohim, not Yahweh or Jehovah. Elohim was apparently the God of the patriarchs, Abraham etc., prior to Moses. It is also clear that the patriarchs worshipped God with various names: El Shaddai (Ex.6:3; Gen 17:1; 43:14 etc.); El 'Elyon (Gen. 14:18-22) El 'Olam (Gen. 21:33); El Ro'i (Gen.16:13); El Bethel (Gen. 31:13/35:7). The Eloist chroniclers tend to use the word God in what we might call a more folksy fashion. He is the Creator, the Everlasting maker of Heaven and Earth. As such he sanctifies specific places, gives and takes away life. It is clear that invoking Elohim was a monotheistic form of address, but the elements of pantheism (worshipping God within his creation) are present in this name. The creation is moved by the Creator, and human history is seen as infused with his power. Human destiny is a manifestation of God. His-story, the working out of God's initial creation through Law, is sacred. Priests, Rabbis, church, temple, mosque institutions receive power by being the legitimate interpreters of sacred His-story. Stories are no longer teachings of how individuals experience De-Light. Sacred stories are the tales of a community of Law as it organizes all life and in the process crushes De-Light.

The dual conception of Yahweh and Elohim as Supreme Ruler and Creator of human destiny is an example of how, by naming god, cultural-historic processes are unleashed. These include the establishment of, and correct use of, the special name. Often a priesthood has been the only sanctioned speaker of the holy name. Armies have often been sent to battle against those who were speaking the name of what was assumed to be a different God. The notion of God as Universal King, Almighty Father, Creator of History carries with it an intolerance which is still accepted as orthodox behavior by modern authorities.

ARE THERE OTHER ACCEPTED CONCEPTIONS OF NAMED GODS?

Another human conception of God is often attributed to the Eleactic school of the ancient Greeks. God is the Divine Principle, that which stands beyond all gods and humans. Originally the Eleatics, and probably many other ancients including Shivites of India, spoke of the Divine Principle as the identity or unity of the universe. This geometric-conception of wholeness has its correspondence in the sign or symbol of the circle. It is found in various forms as the basis of religious language in all pagan cultures. Aboriginal peoples from Australia, South and Central America and Africa hold stories of ancestors who knew and practiced the mathematics of the sacred circle more than 50,000 years ago.

A Catechism for the Children of De-Light

The circle points to totality. It is understood as the ALL. It is the sum of All Being. Once the circle is generated, all other geometric forms are derived by connecting points on the circle with lines. This basic geometric naming of God is still taught by Native Americans, Africans, Australians, Indians, Chinese, Celtic and Germanic peoples. God meaning 'All Is One' is not antithetical to orthodox Jewish doctrine from which Christianity and Islam sprang. But this all-encompassing geometric conception is looked upon as dangerous. For within the circle of unity is implied the whole of Pantheism, what the orthodoxy sees as Nature worship. Unity entails the whole universe, the creation itself being God. Everything is a manifestation of God, if the circle understanding is accepted. In modern discussions many science-oriented ecologists, or people using ecological models and data, speak as if their god is the circle, the All, Unity.

The sacred circle is the name or symbol pointing toward God for another tradition. There existed in the mythology of the Fertile Crescent a person or persons known as Hermes Trismegistus by the Greeks and Thoth by the Egyptians. He may be the same Caucasian, bearded, teacher/holy man known as Viracocha by the Inca. There may have been many of these teachers, their names being an identity of process/way. Through Hermes came knowledge that God was ALL, and more importantly, especially for our time, that ALL was MIND or mental energy. God the Creator was/is a thinker or meditator. All the stuff of the material universe was a product of Mental Projection.

There were/are many schools in the Fertile Crescent, near and far East, the Americas, and the Euro-West which hold MIND/Circle/All/God as the basis from which all emanates. Mystery schools teach that the Great Mystery functions within certain rules of knowledge. Mathematics, the science of numbers, is the key to understanding. Even words and language have rhythmic and symbolic components which can be unraveled revealing the grand organizational plan of the universe. Mystic knowledge is the tool for fulfillment/De-Light. Initiates, through study with Masters, progress along various steps through degrees of symbolic understanding, penetrating the plan of the Great Architect. Through exercise of intelligence one becomes a teacher/priest, the highest human reflection of the secret mysteries. Initiation within these worldwide traditions is oral. Stories are taught which contain the paradoxes that shape human cosmic reality. Since the invention of printing on a mass scale some of these teachings are available in books. But the passing of mystic tradition usually is not recognized unless there is a direct relationship between initiate and teacher/priest(ess).

This God of Super Intelligence, the Mind of the universal All, has become gradually separated with the notion of unity. God is seen as Director, an intelligence outside creation itself. In this form elements of the Great Mind conception of God are found in both Christianity and Islam. Late orthodox Judaism and Kabalistic mysticism also exhibit Mind as giver/receiver of cosmic wisdom. The Mental conception of God has been grounds for some of the bloodiest inquisitions. Pythagorean, Neo-Platonic and Gnostic systems of spiritual knowledge have been the objects of punishments, which often included death for heresy.

The notion of the God Head, the All which is Mind, God being cosmic Consciousness has found wide acceptance in our Aquarian Sub-Age (1840-2015). Like the Greeks and Egyptians or the Hindu, Buddhist and Mayan of another Aquarian Sub-Age cycle (500-311 BCE) we revere the airy, the theoretical, the rational. The reign of science and technology has made it popular for the concept of God to imply mental ordering, mathematical alignments of all material objects, including those of invisible wave energies. That there exists a Supreme Intelligence is perhaps the most universally acceptable image of God in today's industrialized world.

Both the Newtonian world model and the atomic-relativistic world model resulting from Einstein's work offer us evidence of God's mapping and planning. Matter is seen as subject to Universal Laws, which are themselves theoretical-mathematical constructs. As long as God is the Brain behind all reality, as long as He is Supreme and outside the system, manipulating and guiding its course, then the Mental conception of God is acceptable to the Church-Mosque-Temple orthodoxy.

But if that conception of Mind/God becomes too closely connected with the Unity of All, then cries of Pantheism or Deism are heard. The mystical tradition associated with Hermes Trismegistus is protected by the Masonic Order, among others. During the last 130 years the lodges of that order have spread worldwide. Times change, however, and with them the tolerance of the Church, Mosque or Temple. Unless that orthodoxy establishes within its traditions an acceptance of the Concept of God as All or Universal Mind or Ground of Being, we are likely to see after 2015 further attempts to crush the ancient mystical knowledge. God the Father and Ruler, as King and Commander, could well become the only acceptable understanding associated with the speaking of the holy name.

Sensations of continual creation, unity of all life, Total Energy-body Interaction as expressions of cosmic fulfillment are very different from God/Mind conceptions. The later are usually unacceptable to the religious orthodoxy and the corporate dominant culture.

DOES THE ALL OR UNITY CONCEPTION OF GOD DIFFER FROM DE-LIGHT?

God as order gives comfort to rational humans. Geometric patterns are a language that allows us to recognize agreed-upon conceptions. De-Light is different. It is the result of effervescence. It is ever activating. It is the creative process. De-Light results from risking, from going beyond perceived limit. Activating energy is stopped by mental conception, image, pattern. As we attempt to understand, using the tools of language, we create human interpretation of the activating force. Such interpretation is different from sensing the activation itself. So knowledge or understanding of continual creating processes is not possible with any of our languages. We can only, individually experience or sense what makes ongoing life.

Yet, as Children of De-Light we want to speak as if there is Unity, as if ALL is ONE. For when we sense continuous creation everywhere and always it feels like a unifying process. But we must remember that the processes of life creation are of a different order from how we talk of them. The rational ordering of the ALL or the Circle may seem a better way to speak of our De-Lightful experiences, but these are still language limitations, albeit different limitations from those implied by Divine Law, Supreme Ruler, etc.

IS THERE A WAY TO COMMUNICATE OTHER THAN LANGUAGE?

The conception of God as All or Totality, and that conception itself being mental in nature, contains a trick which is the key to all religious language. Mental energy is imagistic. Images, symbols, and signs are the stuff of language. Spoken, written, painted, sculpted, musically sounded, danced, it doesn't matter. The ALL ONE is reflected most keenly through the image-making or Mental process. It is through religious practice, which is itself image-making, utilizing images or idols, that the ALL KNOWING is invoked. Through ceremony, ritual, and magic, humankind comes into harmony with its greater, cosmic potential. We cannot speak of God without the use of human or Mental correspondences. We cannot conceive of ourselves as emanating galactic energies without the galactic image. So in pagan cultures, visioning, imaging and dreaming are processes which are encouraged, for through them we may begin sensing our totality. In Celtic cultures poets/story tellers transmit the ancestral realities, continually bring the world into being through image and rhythm. Native American storytellers occupy a similar position in their communities. The enactment of understanding through a person is different than sacred history passed on in holy books. Intention is different, even though we are using human language capabilities, and our words may sound similar.

Of course the Churches, Mosques and Temples all know this. Their organizations are perpetuated by shaping human consciousness through manipulation of image. They know that there is an individual freedom implied in the Mental image of God. If the spark of the Divine Mind lies within each individual, then the reasons to have religious organizations are very different. A democratic ordering is implied. The hierarchical rule of an ordained, rather than an elected priesthood, is not so relevant if MIND is accessed by all. This freedom from the need for an orthodox form of ritual, ceremony, etc. is yet another reason for crushing any pagan outpourings of reverence.

Experiencing De-Light can happen without image, without organization. Such individual freedom may not even be known by those who control with organized, accepted, dominating power.

HOW ARE MIND AND SPIRIT RELATED?

The circle as a symbolic referent for God/Unity is often identified with the word-conception *SPIRIT*. As *Mind* is a God-concept of all pervasive imagemaking energy in the universe, so *Spirit* is a God-concept of the animating force in the universe. Spirit is the vital essence. Without the creative power of Spirit, the divine influence of God, life would not exist.

The word Spirit is used in both orthodox and pagan cultures as a result of the conquering influence of the dominant Westernizing forces. Yet the actual conception behind this word can be very different for its various speakers. Spirit most often entails the orthodox Creator/Planner/God concept. Spirit can mean continual creation, De-Light, for pagans. These speakings of the same word are done with very different intentions.

There are two notions linked with God Spirit or Great Spirit, which are different from God Mind. One is that Spirit is clearly a necessary element for life. Without it matter would not be alive. The second is that Spirit implies motion within matter. In both cases Spirit is more closely linked with matter than with Mind. Mind is in the realm of ordering. Spirit is imprecise. It is the activator. It is closely linked with emotions like will and intention. Spirit is seen as the Creative; Mind unravels the Plan.

Spirit is seen as behind or outside of creation by the Church, Mosque, Temple priests. Spirit, for them, is like a cause; it happens in an historical past. When it comes through a worshipper, it is viewed with suspicion. Evangelical churches are considered fringe by the orthodoxy.

Spirit for pagans usually indicates ongoing, bubbling-up of creative energies. For pagans, change is perpetual. The Great Spirit, revered in Native American ceremonies, for instance, is a way of conveying the perpetual energy unfoldment of cosmic moments, the Great Flowering.

The Great Spirit or life-giving essence is psychophysical. The Western duality, which separates Mind-Spirit from Body or matter, is not operative for pagans. Great Spirit for us is more like the totality of all vibration. Spirit energy is spoken through story. Experience is Spirit essence. Wisdom based in experience, rather than knowledge based in recorded tradition, is Spirit's expression. The pagan conception of Spirit is very much a way of talking about the experiences of De-Light.

One image of Spirit that allows pagan and orthodox peoples to seemingly communicate in mutually understood celebration is Fire. Fire is the common human experience, the control of fire making us different from other species. Inner fire, our passionate quest for an ever-ongoing-life, is an image reflected for us by campfires and candlelight. The sign of fire may be a crucial beginning for the orthodoxy to begin to realize the vitality in what has been held as pagan, primitive, peasant ways of life.

Inner fire is that which allows us to sense in more than language ways. Immersed within the activating creative forces and sensing these forces through resonance is a more powerful way of communication than any forms of language. Wave energies within the Total Cosmic Energy emanate from within all life forms uniting us. Fires of passion expressed through stories of Gods like Shiva, Dionysus, and Goddesses like Kali and Aphrodite show that materialized or worldly attraction and sexuality are the spark, which continually opens the great mystery. Fire forces which are within mountains, within planetary cores, are also those which continually create Suns. It is a living being's fire that we sense when we feel/know a presence. These fires transcend materiality, space, and time. Such creative energy can seem elusive to rationalist: Trying to capture the source of De-Light can seem like feathers on wind, the effort at snaring merely making the feathers blow further away.

The Church, Mosque, Temple orthodoxy does not like to deal with God as Spirit. Once life-giving vibration is admitted, then it has to be admitted for All Life. If God is Spirit and Spirit is within All Beings, then all of creation is a manifestation of God. That is Pantheism. If this is admitted then life itself becomes sacred, All Life, not just human life functioning within established Divine Laws given only to a chosen few. Because Spirit as the animating life force is invisible, it indicates that there is more going on than meets the eye. It also implies that more is happening than the orthodox organizations would have us believe. In the Spirit realms it is possible that life functions on dimensions different from those of matter. If one part of human life is incorporeal and invisible, then who knows what else might be going on. What is referred to as the Supernatural becomes probable. Immaterial beings such as angels, demons, elves, fairies and disembodied souls or ghosts could be moving in realms all about us. Ancestors might be guiding us. In fact, most people sense these presences at some time during their lives. And pagan cultures base their feelings/understandings about how life unfolds upon these 'extrasensory' sensations.

These realms of Spirit are not usually accepted within the orthodoxies. Historically people practicing interactive Spirit communication have been condemned as witches and wizards and practitioners of the devil's work. To be in touch with the animating life-force energies is to hold potential power, which the orthodox priesthoods can't control. God as Spirit or Great Spirit can be an expression of a cosmology wholly different from one, which is expressed in concepts of God the Father, Ruler of All. Feeling the joy of De-Light can make those who speak with the Divine Authority of the Father upset.

Passionate expressions of Spirit are experiences that are non-linguistic. Great Spirit does not require invocation, for if Great Spirit withdrew itself, creation would cease. Great Spirit requires only appreciation, reverence for life, not obedience to Law. Great Spirit is in and around and throughout everything, every process. Great Spirit is not remote. It did not start and stop. It is life itself. Silence and Darkness are often-times necessary to sense Spirit's presence. Often, once conceptualization happens as we are *in presence*, total resonance stops. The feeling of De-Light snaps. God/Great Spirit is emanation fully sensed, not a concept grasped or a name spoken.

These pagan understandings are in direct contrast to the Christian description of the sacred nature of the Word. The Bible expresses the primacy of language in many places. Words spoken are themselves resonances. But Biblical interpretation of words is in terms of meaning within a framed context. In John 1:1-2 we read "In the beginning was the Word, and the Word was with God, and the Word was God." Once the monotheistic word God is invoked, or once God Himself has spoken, all else is implied, created. The Koran builds upon this power in naming god. Some scholars are certain that the source was Syriac Christianity. *La ilaha illallah*, "there is no God but Allah." To say God or Allah is to imply Law, Order, and Judgement: Very different from Total Energy-body resonance.

IS EXPERIENCING DE-LIGHT THE SAME AS LOVE?

One of the most complex understandings associated with the naming of God is the correspondence with Love. God is Love is the cornerstone of much Christian catechism training and upbringing.

A Catechism for the Children of De-Light

What is implied by Love is an all-caring Father figure, a benevolent and merciful Ruler. But Love is a tricky notion. It is always associated with an outpouring of energy. We know the feeling of nurturing. We learned it in the womb. We experienced it outside the womb as infants. For God to be felt in this way is not to hold Him as untouchable, a remote creator, a universal King. Love, like Spirit, is focused presence.

God understood as Love is not necessarily patriarchal. Relationship, usually involving the tension of gender, is the essence of human love. Love is felt or sensed as being very much a De-Lightful pleasure. Naming God as Love could easily be invoking God the Mother, or god as Mother/Father. God as the Love Spirit brings us through correspondence to the pagan conception of androgynous Father-Mother, King-Queen, creator-instilling paradoxical excitement in All That Is. God in this sense implies the hermaphroditic Center of the Universe from which all else is born. The symbolic circle is unsplit, undivided, contains All. As such it is both the Sun and Full Moon. The beneficent Love God is where the orthodox Church-Mosque-Temple priesthood has to deal most firmly with what they interpret to be idols, often of a sexual nature.

In early Greek Christian practices the word *Agape* became associated with the Love which was God. This word identified the social meal or love feast usually accompanying the Eucharist. The bread and wine sacrament is quite similar to ceremonies performed in the Mythraic and Baccian 'cults' of that period. Here God's ultimate Love is seen in sacrifice. These feasts are rooted in pagan understandings of initiation: Total death of dualism/body, attuned to only five senses/material world attention; replaced by resurrection of attentive, intentional, Total Energy-body awareness, functioning in many dimensional realities at once. The Shivite/Dionysian traditions celebrate death to life with feast and festival. Versions of this practice are in Celtic, African and aboriginal traditions. As the Church consolidated power worldwide it absorbed the symbolic love feast to attract pagans into patriarchal organizations where many immediately felt discomfort. But to stay alive in a conquering dominant condition old traditions were blurred, and eventually often forgotten.

Another Greek Christian understanding of Love centers around the word Eros. Eros in Greek beliefs was the God of Love. He was the son of Aphrodite, and was later the Roman Cupid. Aphrodite was the Greek Goddess of Love and Beauty. She is identified with the Phoenician Astarte and the Roman Venus. All are symbolically born of the foam of the sea. Life on Earth symbolically comes from the oceans, the great planetary womb.

In the accepted religious orthodoxies God as Love is an identification of that Spirit which animates the Christian, Islamic, or Jewish communities. Those communities made of men and women are to share that Love, but not freely. For these are also communities of Law. The Law puts boundaries on Love. Love is allowed conditionally. God therefore inspires Love, which is qualified. Love shared in ritual and ceremony sanctioned by the Church, Mosque, Temple is moral. Loved shared between two humans united in marriage is encouraged. Parental Love resulting from intercourse within marriage is fostered so that the community longevity is assured. All other Love is forbidden. And for those who are truly in the service of God, even sanctioned physical manifestations of Love are forbidden.

The flow of energy associated with Love expressed towards flowers, trees, animals, elements, while revered by the orthodoxy in word and by conferring Sainthood to humans like Saint Francis of Assisi, is squelched by organized actions. Unconditional love of creation and the continual creating forces is usually termed pagan. Love as an expression of De-Light(ful) overflowing is devilish according to the orthodoxies. Gods and Goddesses of Love and Ecstasy are deemed idols. Whole loving cultures have been crushed by the very orthodox institutions, which identify God with Love.

There are two pop culture associations in our time, which are invoked when the name God is spoken. One is the ALL, meaning Mind or Intelligence. The other is LOVE, meaning benevolence or caring. These two understandings of the name God are acceptable in a limited way within the teachings of the Church, Mosque, Temple orthodoxy as it exists within the Pisces great age. In their fullness, however, LOGOS and EROS understandings of the name God point toward very pagan beliefs, which the orthodoxies have routinely crushed.

It is God as Love and Intelligence, which offers us a belief system and a set of habits, which could bring about Earth harmony. God as Supreme ruler sets God apart from creation and leaves the decision-making up to a hierarchy which itself is removed from experiences of De-Light and is promoting global consumption.

Unfortunately, it is God as Supreme Commander, which is the most acceptable understanding among orthodox religions. Decision-making at high levels in our industrial-technological societies is a mimic of military models of a God Who directs, manages and overpowers all obstacles. We are therefore awash in decisions which are short sighted, corrupt, manipulative, and destructive. God as Commander directing Christian, Muslim or Jewish soldiers is not God/Spirit animating all life. These are very different consciousnesses which are often not distinguished, and are therefore prevalent in human cultures in foggy, glossed-over forms.

If the orthodoxies decided to treat ALL LIFE with the reverence of the 'sanctuary/cathedral/temple,' if all life were interacted with daily as the holy of holies, then the current suicidal course on which over consumptive humanity is embarked could be changed. When the orthodoxies say God, wouldn't it be in everyone's best interests if our convictions reflected at-one-ment, total attunement, joy filled expressions of effervescent creation, activating daily manifestations of De-Light?

A Catechism for the Children of De-Light

WHAT DOES DE-LIGHT DO?

Continuous creation is the source of well being for all life. Cellular life on our planet is sensitive to intervention in the normal flow of activator energy. De-Light pulses very much like more familiar wave energies, such as light, sound or radio waves. In mystical traditions De-Light is often termed Divine Light, an image which points toward a source, but doesn't necessarily indicate the activator—continual creation—and may indicate only a visual reality.

Human generated electromagnetic energies interfere with De-Light penetration. Radios, televisions, microwaves used for everything from cooking to communication fill our world with invisible but very powerful force fields which are non natural, in the sense that they are pulsing at rates organized to produce effects for human comfort, resonances different from the basic 10 hertz Earth beat. This din of force is an ever more powerful wall through which De-Light must pass if our senses are to receive continual activation. Much human sickness is attributable to our cellular bodies being overpowered, misaligned, blocked from De-Lightful experiences by the technological marvels that fill our world. Much of the work of the 'Medicine' man or woman, Shaman/Healer is to act as a receiver of De-Light energies, then be a transmitter for those energies in the fields of sickened beings.

A person who is attuned to continual creative force feels like a very bright light, a breath of fresh air, to those who are not so attuned. De-Light pours through such a person. In a world where much of our attention is directed to anti-life—what catastrophe happened or who is killing who—a person emanating De-Light can seem odd, out of place, unlike most people. Yet, animals in the wild will recognize this person right away as one of them. Birds, fish, trees, all kinds of plants will freely interact with such an attuned human. All our Kin, all the species of life on this planet in addition to humans, are under human attack, their sensitivities are being bombarded with modern technologies, intentionally or unintentionally. Their illnesses are in great part do to blockages of De-Light as humans construct realities.

A Catechism for the Children of De-Light

Practitioners of De-Light speak of it being high, as opposed to low energy. As we come into this material existence we become entwined with matter. Matter is much slower energy. It forms. It forms shapes we recognize as this material world. We slow to experience what it is like to live the material, matter filled, existence. Continual creation—De-Light—from our form-based perceptions, is much speedier. When material bodies 'die' they merge with De-Light. Practitioners of De-Lightful life awareness attempt to retain as much as possible of the faster pre- and post-material existence creative forces. We do not wish to be pulled in or down, drowned by the temporary manifestation as a material body in a world of material bodies. We seek out others who retain much of their De-Light energy fulfillment. Many of these others are not human. Animals, plants, insects, fungi, microorganisms emanate De-Light, as do free streams of water, winds, devas, angels, fairies, ancestors—the non-human essences of Earth life, sometimes seen, often unseen but sensed as presences among which we are never alone.

Awareness in decision-making based on Part 1

1. Your words contain cosmologies.
2. Which and whose cosmologies are you speaking?
3. Where we focus our attention determines who we are and how we act.
4. Creation happens in every moment.
5. Laws limit.
6. Language(s) define.
7. Sensing De-Light.

PART II
PRINCIPLES OF
CORRESPONDENCE/
REFLECTION

"As above, so below; as below, so above."
— The Kybalion —

A Catechism for the Children of De-Light

WHAT IS THE FORM OF THE ALL, THE ONE, DE-LIGHT?

De-Light creates. Creation is recognizable as forms, shapes, familiar sounds, patterns. All our attempts at understanding creation start with human limitation. We are confined by our senses, (sight, hearing, touch, smell, and taste) and by our sensibilities or capabilities for perception and feeling. Most importantly, languages themselves are limitations. What cannot be spoken, written, painted, played or danced lies beyond human conception. The instant we attempt to apprehend, we are structuring. We may be acknowledging apparent order, but such recognition is an act of organizing on our parts.

Any linguistic formation, sign or symbol, is therefore given meaning as a result of belief. Languages are able to convey information because of the user's attitude of acceptance. That words or symbols or signs mean anything at all implies trust. Belief, acceptance and trust are basic to all communication.

Words or symbols or signs become elements of habit due to common usage. If when you say God you mean Supreme Being, you have established a habit in your perception. If you mean Creator, another habitual pattern is present. Saying Great Spirit or De-Light sets another distinct pattern in our understandings. In religious language it is these habits of language usage which solidify and become objects to be defended. Rather than recognizing points of view, more often than not one point of view becomes dogma. That dogma becomes orthodox. All other uses of the language then become wrong.

I direct the reader to this awareness of limitation, because it is especially crucial in the following discussion of what is often termed the second Hermetic Law, the Law of Correspondences. This law is usually stated: as above, so below; as below, so above. The law assumes agreement that the universe operates according to recognizable pattern, that God is MIND, an ordering source. Without knowing it, one or another form of this law is implied in most of our attempts at understanding anything about life.

A Catechism for the Children of De-Light

WHAT IS MEANT BY 'ABOVE'?

Simply stated we are apparently presented with a two dimensional view of the universe. Above means Up. Below means Down. These are special directives. This primitive view of special reality is very difficult for sophisticated, scientific human beings to accept, yet it permeates all our languages. We might substitute the words "As out there, so in here; as in here, so out there." Then we should understand that the outer reaches of space are no different than what is here on our planet. Another way to put it might be to say, "the universe is in the atom; the atom is the universe." The greatest expanse of matter we can conceive is also our smallest conception. Universe and atom are One. The harmony is symbolized by the circle within the circle.

Our languages are rich, and a total description of Matter in Space offers only a partial description of our reality. We can talk of the condition of that matter. We have just done so by drawing the circle within the circle image. What is outside us are apparent forms of order. Perceptions of ordering and Law penetrating the greater universe reflect our own abilities to perceive. What is out there functions with Mental energies like our own. The All is mathematical. It is the generator of Principle. Universal ordering is itself made up of recognizable Forms. We might say that the Universal All is a Language, which allows us the possibility of understanding ambitions of a Greater Understanding.

But what is out there is not simply Matter and Mental Forms. Vitality, Life, the Living Force is through the ALL just as it is here in all beings on the earth. Without that Spirit, De-Light, the All—the agreed upon totality—is dead. The animating force, what Jung called the anima , is just as much the source as it is the totality.

For the pagan, this correspondence between Greater and Smaller is the cornerstone of belief, as creation becomes form. For if the All in its totality can be understood by perceiving similarities here in our earthly condition, then this life is no less sacred than that Life. What has become dualism in the West, separating Matter from Mind-Spirit, is not dualism for the pagan. There exists a fundamental unity in All Creation. The Creator is not the Mind or Spirit outside the Material World setting it in motion (Deism) and taking no interest in it. Nor is the Creator a personal Counselor moving Matter in an act of Will. The Creator is the whole of, and within all of Creation as a continually effervescent producer of potential form. It is the De-Light (ful) energy which we call the ALL, manifested materially, mentally, and spiritually. It is holy, sacred, throughout creation.

WHAT HAPPENS WHEN THE ALL IS SPLIT APART?

If all Matter or Materiality is understood as different from what is of the Mind or of the Spirit (as it has been in the West since the philosophers Leucippus and Democritus in Greece), then the proper sign for God and Creation would be two circles side by side.

The stuff of the Spirit or Mind is then considered Higher or Holy, while the stuff of Materiality is considered Lower or Mundane. The wedge of this separation is driven deeper until all earthly considerations are seen as endangering to what is whole. Thus the human body became the seat of temptation, the fallen source of evil. Assertions that what is physical must be cleansed and lifted beyond the material or earthy to find unity with the sacred are made even by those who claim to understand the principle of correspondences.

Often correspondences are only between higher human manifestations and the Heavenly. Here the duality, which separates matter away from the ALL, is present. It is this separation which is a key element in the acceptable belief structures of the Church, Mosque, Temple complex. Hindu and Buddhist have become acceptable to the orthodoxy or dominant cultures of the West and Middle East because they apparently maintain the duality, which separates Materiality from Mind-Spirit. Within those Eastern traditions, however, many maintain no division, that merging with the ALL is merely direction within the world of matter, an inevitability which none can escape.

A Catechism for the Children of De-Light

HOW IS THE UNITY OF THE GREATER AND THE SMALLER REFLECTED IN MATTER?

There are many examples of the small circle within the larger circle among all the living things of earth. The eye, the process of flowering, a spider's webbing are but a few of these reflections. These correspondences or reflections are understood as teachers by pagans. Teachers are everywhere. De-Light comes through all life and is reflected as circular form coming from a center. Plant stems, trees trunks, veins and arteries, rushing streams also mirror this reflection. Unity and creating activity is everywhere in nature on this Earth. There are no natural reflections of the dualistic, split circle, outlook, however. Dualism, i.e. separation of Mind-Spirit from Physical bodies, is a human projection on a De-Light(ful), unified, process.

Dualism may come from human fear and therefore a need to control. To experience De-Light is to remain open to all that is. This nakedness requires that as you are creative in life so you allow all of creation to freely move through you. If you look toward the universe and see God as a first cause, as a Father or Mother, greater than yourself, different than all creation, then this hierarchical projection is mirrored in your everyday life, in how you speak and think. All the beings of Earth will seem lesser, lower, dirtier. Earth processes of bodily expression will be repressed, hidden, closed. What will be most holy, most sacred, are the aspects of human life which mirror your conception of God, in this case remoteness, separation from material reality. All natural processes will need to be controlled, manipulated, redirected.

How you understand correspondences is how you make decisions about life. The orthodox, dominant culture of monotheists acts as though duality is reflected everywhere in life. The pagan acts with De-Light, feeling the oneness, the unity of ALL everywhere in life. One of the primary reasons for expressing these principles is to communicate this distinction to those who occupy the decision-making tables. Currently, the civilizing forces of the dominant culture consider their mission within the Laws

A Catechism for the Children of De-Light

of their God(s) to dominate the processes of Earth. Are salmon, cranes, trees more important in all of creation as an expression of continual creative De-Light than motor boats, paper, streams damned for electricity? Ask yourself which side you are on. You can't be on both.

What is implied in these questions is perhaps the most crucial distinction between pagan and orthodox viewpoints. To the pagan, consciousness understanding is not determined by or dependent upon language/conceptions. Natural order is not projections of the higher MIND. On the other hand, within the orthodoxy, all understanding is linguistic; and thus language expressions are limited to humans. Languages of Dolphins, Wolves, Birds, are curious, but are not considered as reflections of the sacred Word. One of the great problems of Western philosophy was entertained by Bishop Berkeley: if a tree falls in a forest and there is no one there to see it, does it actually fall? If the answer is no, the tree doesn't fall, then it is obvious that life is understood as human projection. If the answer is yes, it does fall, what is implied? One answer is a nonhuman-oriented natural process. Life would happen regardless of humans. But the trick in asking his question is, that the second we humans attempt to comprehend the process of the tree falling, then it becomes a linguistic product of our thinking. So all understanding remains synthetic, in the sense that language is a function of habit/belief, learned in social contexts which are the manifestations of historical human interactions.

The orthodoxy has a narrow definition of language. It might seem very broad to us when we realize that it includes all cultural languages. It also includes all that is written, spoken, signed and symbolized. Language is also inclusive of all that we call the arts, painting, sculptor, design, dance, music, etc. In short, all the possible means of human communication are covered by what is considered acceptable language.

Pagan consciousness, however, recognizes that there are other languages. Birds, Dolphins, Plants, Rocks and Trees all talk. All beings, animate and inanimate, communicate. Humans are not uniquely communicators. All of Creation is alive in something like a linguistic fashion. The signs and symbols of that language exist everywhere and are instantaneously available all the time. The pagan does not see natural communication as a product of human projection. What we hear, when we listen, is not human noise, or form, it is not an anthropomorphized world, a mirroring of human centeredness, a narcissistic wonderland. Instead it is understood that each being is projecting its peculiar sense of ordering. Each of these ways of ordering is an attempt to express effervescent, creative De-Light. Our humble task as human beings is to attempt to comprehend all that is there for us to understand. We need to learn all these other languages, hear their expressions of oneness, share their senses of De-Light. Our goal is not management of life, but ever greater sensitivity to the life-creating processes.

As sensitive pagans, Hermetic correspondences are somewhat different than is commonly described within human languages. The closed circle sign, meaning the ALL or Great Spirit or God or De-Light is only a human, geometric form. The rock's roundness is less geometrically perfect: after all, a perfectly round rock is rare. Rocks speak with a tendency toward roundness. That roundness expresses the harmony, which is explosions, weathering, geologic displacement. Rocks are not God or gods, but they do correspond to the quiet wholeness, which is always and everywhere the given natural order.

Sensitive pagans see correspondences, the smallest within the greatest, everywhere in nature. The watery eye is the easiest example. Eyes of humans, birds, cats, dogs, bears, rabbits, mice, salmon, all eyes on all beings emanate or speak of the Spirit of ALL, of De-Light, of the anima of Creation. As we humans look deep into the eyes of any creature, we know oneness. We know KINSHIP. We know all life is sacred. In that moment of looking, De-Light is shared. Moths and butterflies, dragonflies and other insects exhibit eyes on their wings. These too are signs of the oneness, as are spores, fungal spots on leaves, all of which often appear as a small roundness within a greater roundness.

DOES SHARING DE-LIGHT MEAN THAT ONE BEING SHOULD NOT KILL ANOTHER?

Death on earth corresponds to stars in nova, galaxies spinning outward beyond recognizable pattern, material realities coming into form in space/time only to change form again and again until that form is not identifiable. Death is seen by us bodily. Continual creation must be fed, like fire. Stars need gases to burn to glow. They consume those gases. Bacteria need fungi or other mediums on which to feed. As above, so below. Matter consumes other forms of matter in the process of creating itself, sustaining itself, and eventually being consumed by other forms of matter, other beings. Death is as much De-Light as Life is. Continual becoming is continual going away, often into other recognizable processes, which become forms.

To look, eye to eye, then to kill, is a process that animal, insect, even plant and microbial species share. Predation, which leads to one life becoming another life, is within the unity, the ALL. Pagans tend to understand this process by being part of it, if their sustenance is still one with other beings and the land. However, as the world has industrialized, as people have moved into cities, as food has become a commodity to be purchased and consumed, few of these people have probably shared the killing/ death experience.

Instead killing is a remote process, one that happens in food factories, or in wars, or in twisted emotional outbursts, that have nothing at all to do with sustenance, a continual creation life force activity. In fact, as most people rely on others to do killing for them to survive, death in one's own life is often feared. That fear generates energy blockages, shutting off open sensitivity to De-Light.

ARE OTHER CORRESPONDENCES CRUCIAL TO PAGAN UNDERSTANDING?

Much can be learned through death. Modern scientist, like many ancient peoples, examine cross-sections, which reveal the small within the great design. The smallest plant, the largest tree, when cross-sectioned reveals the fluid passageways and ringed growth, from the center outward. The formative language of plant life, recorded in its structure, speaks of the All within the one.

A fundamental unity between all animal and plant life is expressed through similarities of bones, stems, trunks. Cross sectioned, they look and function somewhat the same. Vessels of life are living signs of the ALL. Each is, even in death, a trace or a track of where life has been. For these reasons bones, feathers, etc. are revered as teachers, reminders, by pagan peoples. They are not idols, nor are they merely decorations. They are elements of natural language.

One of the primary correspondences, which is below as it is above, is the darkness of Space itself. All openings on the Earth have a similar quality. Caves, natural passageways into rock, are only potentially receptive of Light. They exist with rock, earth harmony, but they are open for potential, for birth, for occupation. The correspondence of caves or deep recesses to the deep, unknown sources of continual creation makes these places particularly sacred to pagan peoples. Lodges built for human occupation often mimic these natural openings. The mud and grass earth lodge is rounded as a reflection of caves, which are a reflection of the domed sky as we look out toward the stars. Teepees, hogans, African and other tropical dwellings, quite often mimic the cave.

The vagina and womb of female animals, the receptacles of flowers, are all seen as reflections of the cosmic dark, the place where De-Light becomes life and Light. Female De-Light expressed in rolling orgasms and birthing reflects cosmic generation, the continual bang, turning energy into form.

A Catechism for the Children of De-Light

Perhaps the most important correspondence of the pagan understanding is recognized as that of the Sun disk with the cosmic winged form.

Often this disk is shown as winged, its relationship with high birds such as the eagle being quite obvious. The Sun is the Light and Life provider for all Earthly life. Without it there would be only darkness. Even the moon would have nothing to reflect, only darkness.

The Sun itself is understood by pagans to have an Earthly correspondence, that being Fire. Fire of all kinds is an element of generative force. It consumes all, returning any material form to gases, eventually to the source, thereby being an earthly reminder of De-Light. Fire is always in correspondence with Great Spirit, Oneness, Unity. It is also seen as corresponding to vitality, the creative life force itself.

When the roundness of life is filled with spirit or fire, potential is realized, forms elongate. This correspondence is stated geometrically as the process of ellipse. An ellipse is a plane curve such that the sum of the distances from any point of the curve to two fixed points, called a foci, is a constant. In solid geometric terms, it is a section of a cone.

'As above'— in the heavens—the solid, round bodies are in motion. This motion is a relationship of two, as in our Sun and its orbiting planets. The orbits, the traces of these moving bodies, are not round but elliptical. These heavenly bodies, as they wobble on their axis, also trace elliptical patterns. (The period of this wobble for Earth is 26,000 years and is known as 'precession of the equinoxes' also as the 'Platonic' or 'great year.') These movements are the key to generation and life on the material plane. Gender, male and female, is introduced into the elliptical correspondence. It takes two derived from one to bring about material life. And those two must exhibit motion.

This principle is spoken clearly for us everywhere on earth. All animal bodies exhibit elongation. All plants, flowers, petals, leaves, blades of grass are elongated ellipsoids.

A Catechism for the Children of De-Light

Most seeds are elliptical in form, exhibiting potential growth. Eggs are elliptical spheroids. Their cracking with new birth is the sign of material Life regeneration. Many fruits and vegetables are elliptical spheroids, exhibiting that they are seed bearers. So are cones on pines. So are nuts. Many anatomical parts of animals speak the elliptical language. Eye sockets, lips, ears, external genital openings, male penises, finger nails, hooves, the teachers are everywhere.

Even fire, as a flame in a candle, exhibits elliptical potential. The elliptical language tells the pagan that life is happening. Regeneration is in progress. Vitality, De-Light is manifesting.

What is outside is inside. What is in the Heavens is on Earth. The All is in the smallest grain of sand or grain seed. Correspondence between Heaven and Earth is everywhere apparent. Not only is the Heavenly Holy, so are all the manifestations of Heaven on Earth.

Awareness in decision-making based on Part II

1. Communication implies trust.
2. In immediate events (the small), we can understand the grander order (the great).
3. Belief in duality is destructive.
4. Our teachers are everywhere.

PART III
PRINCIPLES OF
VIBRATION/RELATIONSHIP

"It moves. It moves not. It is far, and it is near. And it is outside of all this."
— Upanishads —

WHAT IS VIBRATION?

"Twinkle, Twinkle Little Star, How I wonder What You are?" With fascination we look to the heavens. The twinkling we perceive as we gaze at stars and planets is one of our earliest reminders that everything is in motion. Great and slow motions of the Sun and Moon effect earth life from the outside. Vibratory motion, effervescent continual creative outpouring is within ALL material forms. The way we differentiate between the various manifestations of the ALL ONE is through perception of varying rates and modes of vibration. Movement of the life force shapes, causes form, allows for visual recognition. Where vibratory motion changes and life in a form leaves to become another, less recognizable form, we say death has occurred. Life force is motion.

De-Light, pouring forth into form, fills that form. A filled form is in tension. Forms do not go beyond their recognizable selves until they cross the life ending moment at death. The tension that is identified as a life interacts with other tensions that are identified as other lives. Humans, trees, animals, insects, planets, flowers, all emit and contribute to a kind of pressing, plucking, stroking of each others tensions. Vibration is a physically descriptive term. The Physicist defines vibration as a periodic, usually rapid oscillatory motion of an elastic or rigid body suddenly released from tension. This release can be measured. Vibrations can then be seen as wave motions; field energies showing variations in amplitude or intensity.

All matter, all being, all mind, all spirit, is energy. All that IS exists in a condition of stretching. De-Light pushes outward, ever creating. All energies are pushed and pulled by themselves and interactions with other energies, simultaneously. At any moment, a stretched or extended or strained condition appears rigid to the human observer. We sense solid form. Because of the principle of polarity (to which we will turn in another section) the stretched condition is pulled in yet other directions. The release of that tension in one of those directions sets a flow of energy going in that different direction. As this action happens over and over at very rapid rates, a recognizable pulse, a vibration is set up.

We are most keenly aware of this principle in the realm of musical instruments. The stretched string is plucked or bowed, setting up a vibration which is within our auditory range capabilities and is heard as a tone. The drum, the vibrating reed, the lip in the mouthpiece of a trumpet or used to blow air across the opening in a flute, exhibit the vibratory function for us. In each case, it is two or more tensions interacting that produce a release, a tone. Relationship of two or more vibrating entities appears necessary for tension release. Tension release is crucial to the experience of De-Light because it is how new vibrations, new energy forms, are created and released. It is the process of continual creation.

All tension releases are celebrated by pagans as sacred. Two human bodies stroking each other, bringing about orgasm are in a condition of De-Light. A person bringing sound from their voice box or from an instrument is in a condition of De-Light. Similarly, birds singing, wolves howling, whales emitting high pitched melodies are all in conditions of De-Light.

Different entities vibrate at different rates. Interactions of entities release vibrations of differing amplitudes. These measured motions are spoken of as the momentum of that entity. Momentum is the product of the mass and the velocity of that entity. Obviously, the momentum of a planet will be quite different from that of a cell, if they are both calculated to be moving at similar velocities in space. Two beings moving at similar rates of speed and having similar mass are likely to exhibit similar vibrations. With this principle we differentiate between individual entities. We identify individuals, and classes of individuals. A turtle is like other turtles but is vibrationally different from an electron. The energy pattern of a thought is different from the pattern emitted by a rock.

IS VIBRATION EVERYWHERE THE SAME KIND OF ENERGY?

Using the principle of correspondence, vibratory motion is everywhere alike. The tension of planets moving in orbit around their suns is involved with their spinning on their axis. It is believed that the suns move around other central points of energy as a result of a great tension moving outward, that motion being galactic, the galaxies spinning around each other and in a great stretching. Atoms, of which molecules are made, also exhibit continual motion, or so it appears when we measure their traces. Even atoms, made up of protons (having a positive charge), electrons (carrying an negative charge) and neutrons (electrically neutral) are in a state of very rapid vibration, so rapid that their movement is not called motion. At this most basic level of our vibratory universe, the tension, or at-rest quality, is spoken of as a tendency or probability pattern.

This tension-stretching of the vibratory universe, coupled with the notion of probability-pattern, introduces us to an understanding that flexibility, rather than rigidity, prevails through-out our universe. All entities exhibit the tendency to return to their original shapes once they have been pushed or pulled into deformation. Those shapes themselves embody vibratory patterns. As humans, we grow to trust those patterns. We believe they are stable. We refer to these patterns as Reality. If the tendency toward elasticity were not present in the Universe, then vibrations could be totally random and chaotic. Elasticity, or trusted vibratory patterning, is the basis for a belief in natural order.

IS ELASTICITY, THE TENSION-STRETCHING ITSELF A MEDIUM?

Does the vibratory nature of the ALL exist as a link between matter and energy or force? Is De-Light identifiable as the materializing stuff-process which holds reality together? These are not necessarily questions formed of the dualistic split between Matter and Energy. However, in the West, where Matter is separated from Mind-Spirit, the dualism is often latent in these questions.

For the pagan consciousness, however, vibration is the medium of transmission through which matter becomes energy or energy becomes matter. This transmission has to do with speeding up or slowing down. It is the essence of the alchemical notion of transmutation. One entity changing into another.

In some occult understandings vibratory elasticity is the grounds for postulation of an Ethereal Substance. This Ether is Matter at a higher degree of vibration. This elevated matter fills all Space. It is the stuff between vibrating entities such as atoms and other minute corpuscles.

To most pagan understanding, however, vibration itself fills the void. There is no space between bodies in relationship. All space is filled with vibrating, creating, De-Lightful energies. Each body sends outward its peculiar vibration. What exists outside a vibrating entity is a myriad of other vibrating entities, all coming from their creative centers, a sea of De-Light(ful) relationships.

Our job, as conscious humans consists of selecting from the continual bombardment of vibratory patterns as we receive them. This is what the pagan means by Attunement. We recognize another probable pattern, within all the available vibrations, by remembering what that entity felt like in previous recognition. They may be visually disguised. We still sense who they are.

Attuning to other vibrating sources requires attention. Attention is itself a focusing of mental, pattern recognition energy. When we pay attention to vibration we learn its probable pattern. Stars in this galaxy and galaxies beyond ours exhibit certain similarities of light, heat, magnetic and radio wave energies. Planets are different vibrations from suns. Some like ours are watery. Some are dry. Some are frozen. Different kinds of gases form in relation to those vibratory conditions and those gases themselves are of various wavelengths. Water has a vibrational pattern which when heated can turn to vapor and gas, but when cooled can turn to ice. Plankton and fish exhibit vibratory patterns, which allow them to survive within the water pattern. Atmospheric gaseous patterns alone would be toxic to the grasses. Trees require the water vibration, but in limited amounts. A plant's requirement is for living earth, the vibrational patterns of which are governed by the presence of bacteria, protozoa, yeasts, etc. devouring each other and themselves—motions in a probable pattern. The soil minerals required by these microbes are themselves identifiable as energy patterns.

Birds and cats listen for their prey. Birds of a feather vibrate together, and quite suddenly rise or dive, as one being. Each individual being emits a vibrational pattern, which is recognizable by other beings. Elk sense when they are around other elk creatures or in a condition where they are not threatened. Their herd vibration is very intense. A sensitive, attuned being, a human or a wolf, can pick up that pattern from far away. When a predatory creature enters the vibrational range of sentinel elk, the whole herd immediately changes their stance, their emission patterns. Pagan hunters know how to attune themselves to the elk vibration and many other creatures on which they depend for food, clothing and shelter. The kill is sacred, because it happens within the vibrational attonement, if done properly.

All beings emit a vibrational pattern that can be received by other attuned beings. Humans can adjust their patterns to merge with certain patterns of others. Humanness, our human vibration, is not lost when fine-tuning how we are to be among our Kin on this world.

WHAT ARE MEDICINES?

Humans and other animals know that certain plants emit vibrations that are able to offset sickness. Sickness can be seen or felt as a diminished emission of probable patterning from a being. To rejuvenate that flow, vibrations from other beings are ingested. Plant's particularly strong vibrational qualities are often referred to as herbs.

A Catechism for the Children of De-Light

The touch of a healer is the intended emission of intensified vibrations aimed at offsetting vibrations that have for whatever reason dwindled. Injury to a body changes the quality and quantity of energy emission from that body. A healer's vibrations are strong enough to overpower shrinking or sickened conditions.

Humans have learned over the millennia that vibrational patterns are reflected in how creatures move, how they dance. Pagan peoples see that one human seems to feel like a buffalo bull feels. Another like a rabbit. Others like birds or fish. Many tribal people take-on the character of an animal, bird, insect or plant in ceremony conveying stories of that vibrational characteristic so that others can understand. Among Native Americans, Africans, natives of Australia, India, Lapland and elsewhere community is understood as a collection of these medicines or animal perceiving, ways, movements. Not only does the council of beings, acting through humans, bring about tolerance but an experience of reverence, as humans in these cultures interact with kinship of all. Reverence for individual differences reflects the basic relationships of the universe.

These vibrational patterns, differing species to species, are not considered strict; they are elastic, probable. They can and do change. Medicine dancers often reflect a complex character, a bird or other animal, and an element like clay or wind, painted and molded in one mask. The Kachina dancers of their Southwest United States tribes are a good example.

This vibration-animal-knowledge is even extended to how we understand patterns reflected in the stars. Constellations look like various animal figures. No such patterns actually exist. But over time ancient cultures found that the positions of certain groupings of stars relative to the human position on earth reflected vibratory qualities throughout a given cycle of earth life. Thus, when Leo, the Lion's energy is prominent for a period of time (or in a person), Lion-like vibrational qualities (kingliness, regale, self-centeredness) are dominant. These vibrational correspondences define patterns repeated over and over in cycles of human experience. The basis of astrological knowledge is learned vibrational energy, defined through perceived differences between vibrations in relationship.

WHAT HAPPENS WHEN A VIBRATIONAL QUALITY DISAPPEARS?

Absence of a particular probable vibration associated with an entity is death. Most obviously, a carcass has vibrations, but it is those associated with beings that bring about decay and decomposition of material bodies. For the same reason ceremonial masks and clothing implants placed in museums as art objects do not emit their intended vibrational qualities. Ceremonies themselves can become carcasses of no vibrational power if those practicing the ceremony or some in attendance are emitting no-De-Light (ful) vibrations. The creative process is not in the object unless the object is involved in that creativity.

Less obvious to most people are humans (and possibly other beings) who exhibit only vibrational wave energies of greed, fear, and/or conquest. Although these humans are walking they appear dead to attuned pagans because they are not emitting normal, probable-patterning. Instead they emit vibrations that feel hostile or defensive or parasitic. Such projections are dangerous. Anger, fear, hostility projected into a world of Kin disrupts. A mob or society emitting this kind of vibrational energy can overpower any individual or group of individuals emitting gentler energy. Vibrational warfare is infectious in the sense that it dampens, brings down De-Light (ful) energy. Only with continually applied attention and intention to generation of creative De-Light can De-Light shine in vibrational darkness and storm.

Many cultures have created practices for keeping De-Light alive. Individual practices of meditation and yoga and vision questing are all taught for this purpose. Community and group practices of ceremony and ritual movement work to keep continual creativity happening.

A Catechism for the Children of De-Light

Pagans know that an ailing body, a sick body, is one in which the vibratory patterning has begun to shift toward physical death. As all of the elements of that physical entity are in vibration, what is needed in every case is a return to proper probable-patterning, a vibrational adjustment. All elements of that physical entity, including the thought vibrational adjustment, have to be in harmony if the being is to be healthy. Vibratory patterning which is not attuned to its own normalcy is also improperly placed in the total environment. Total environmental health requires returning all entities, all conditions, to their normal, natural, probable patterning. Industrial-technological interference must be vibrationally (vibration ally) attuned (maybe silenced) for total environmental balance to occur.

When entities reflect sickness (often sickness they take-on because of the imbalance of their living situations or their environment) those entities must be adjusted, healed, for they are affecting all beings. Humans in a vibrationally damaging condition can often right that condition by becoming aware of its source. Its source is always a tension, a stress, which is foreign to the normal elasticity, therefore producing an out of balance vibratory rate. Recognition is itself a powerful vibration. Recognition of proper pattern, done habitually, can, often does, offset habits of vibrational sickness. If that does not work, then other vibrational tools can be used. Herbs, the healing hands of a shaman, placing the sick person in a totally healthy environment, all can bring about wellness. Out of balance vibrations can be speedy; but they can be redirected by very centered equally fast, healthy, De-Light (ful) vibrations. Often, sickness manifests as a slowing of vibration, a dragging. This is usually accompanied by the entity swirling inward, like a whirlpool vortex, becoming self-consuming. To reverse this vibration, they must receive energy enough to begin swirling outward, reversing the vortex in which they have trapped themselves, for whatever reason.

When Herbs, or synthesized versions of 'medicines,' are introduced to sickened individuals there is danger. Each of these introductions itself sends out vibratory information. The physical effect of these synthesized medicines is often akin to poisoning. The entity is speeded up by a rush of cells to overcome an invader. Or, in the case of introducing herbal vibrations, the body is aligned with that plant's vibration. In either case, it is very easy for an individual's probable vibrational patterning to be altered in ways that can merely bring about a different kind of 'sickness.' The drugged condition must be eliminated if a human, animal or plant or microbe is to regain its own probable vibrational patterning. This is why pagan healers will usually try adjusting the vibrational rate through song, ritual, dance, etc. before vibrations of plants are introduced. Synthetic drugs are a last resort, because it is known that they leave behind as much or more damage, vibrationally, than they overpower.

All bodies are vibratory instruments. They can be quickened, and therefore expanded in capability, or they can be slowed down, deadened. The current vibratory situation on our planet is one filled with poison and sickness. All beings are suffering. Industrial vibrations are hard, metallic, loud, generating background vibrational pollution that has itself become so familiar to humans that normal vibrational qualities seem 'boring' too quiet, fear producing. The roar of trucks, planes, trains, cars, factories, is so pervasive that all beings adjust. Subtler vibratory pollutants such as repeated, loud, rhythmic language and visuals used by advertisers over radio, television and movie waves, actually mesmerize normal energy patterning to an extent that normalcy is not wanted by vast majorities of humans. People are vibrationally sluggish as they appear to speed around in their cars, computers, airplanes. They have little contact with other beings, other vibrational Kin on this planet, living lives encased in air conditioning and cement, surrounded by others who are identical to themselves.

In this industrial-technological era a few humans with pagan consciousness have sought to remove themselves from the vibratory clatter that has become the accepted norm. Perhaps a few of those people are readers of this book, but since reading is not a primary, vibrational, experience, only De-Light (ful) experience itself is capable of increasing the rate of probable human vibration. This speeding-up of the human receptor-sender cannot be instantaneous. Drug tripping does not enhance the instrument. It is the slow experiencing, De-Light (ful) repetition, which lasts. All the vibratory elements of the human entity are involved. If we were to try to describe this experience it might look something like the following: A human body revolves slowly. It turns round and round, but its speed does not break the air enough to create noise. Then the movement is increased in velocity. The body whirls. Like Dervishes of Persia, the body creates a rush of air, making a sound pass the ears of the listener. Then the human body begins adjusting that air-sound with its breath. A vocal accompaniment to the whirling body moves from a low vibratory note. All the notes of the musical scale(s) accompany the ever faster whirling of the body. At last the whirling is so rapid that the musical notes go past audible levels for humans. As the body spins faster and faster wave energies become perceptible. First emissions of heat can be observed. These waves change color, beginning with red, becoming orange, then yellow, then green, blue, indigo, violet, then color disappearing, or becoming a blinding white light coming from within the speeding body.

Gradually the body turns into white light rays, becoming like electric magnetic radiation of extremely short wavelengths, or X-rays. When even higher vibrations are attained, electrical and magnetic rays are emitted, and beyond that molecular structures disintegrate, and there is a merging with the ALL, total UNITY, total De-Light.

Children of DE-LIGHT often move through the world with such vibrational awareness. As long as s/he remains in the physical body, the limits of the molecular structure's vibratory rates are not totally surpassed. But in states of deep meditation, or attunement during ceremony, the vibrating entity leaves the body behind and journeys through the earth world and into other vibratory dimensions of the total universe. When the entity returns, the body is rejuvenated.

A Catechism for the Children of De-Light

Because of such De-Lightful experiences pagans move freely with all the beings of earth and with invisible entities whose vibrations are speedier than those currently accepted as normal by most people. Fairies, devas, gnomes, angels, all exist at vibratory levels slightly outside the realm of material reality.

In a condition of De-Light there is no split between matter and spirit or mind. Without this split ordained priesthoods of all kinds have a difficult time justifying their interpretive powers. The dominant orthodoxies do not encourage humans to understand the principles of vibration. Instead they emphasize the role of doctors, psychologists, those who work within frameworks that require expertise in how to adjust to the dominant culture's way of controlling what is natural. Healthy, vibrationally attuned, humans, are generally feared by the dominant culture. De-Light is recognized only as actions that are out-of-step with hierarchical, conquering, forces. Ironically, what appear to be the civilizing forces, those which overpower natural vibration, are the destabilizing forces. These are principled only with laws that disrupt unity. Principles of De-Light, vibrational wholeness and health, should be seen as how humanity lives with all vibrating realities. That kind of principled living would constitute a positive civilizing contribution by humans.

Awareness in decision-making based on Part III

1. Tensions provoke resonance.
2. Life resonates.
3. Quality of resonance reveals vitality.
4. All interactions are vibrational.

PART IV
PRINCIPLES OF POLARITY, CONTRARIES, and CHANGE

"The 'this' is also 'that', The 'that' is also 'this.' That the 'that' and the 'this' cease to be opposites is the very essence of Tao. Only this essence, an axis as it were, is the center of the circle responding to the endless changes."
— Chuang Tzu —

WHY IS THERE APPARENT POLARITY?

Because manifestations of the ALL are in motion, there appears to be polarity. All material beings, all emotions, all thoughts, everything that makes up reality as we understand it exists in relationship to at least one other. These relationships which are always moving, allow us to perceive difference. Some differences are very slight; some so extreme as to seem to be set off—opposite—appearing to be not what the other is. Everything that is exists as a collection of relationships, which themselves manifest as extremes. For this reason any identifiable life form appears to 'have two sides,' exhibiting opposition. All manifestations of De-Light show as two aspects, the extreme held in tension by the unity which is recognizable by humans. Life appears as paradox, resolved in the Oneness of the ALL or TAO.

HOW DO EXTREMES HAPPEN?

Cosmic vibrations manifest as rotation or spinning in the smallest particle and the largest galaxy. Stars (suns) and planets move in interactive tension. Modern science has reconstructed this understanding which we share with many ancient cultures.

Earth (or any planet) is in effect a magneto. It displays the effects of two poles at either extremity of a line of direction passing through its mass (its axis). The properties of one end of that pole carry a charge, which is opposite to those at the other end of that pole. North Pole and South Pole are points where opposite forces or qualities are concentrated. These are points of maximum intensity. The magnetic fields, which blanket the earth, meet at these zero degree points. Because of rotation between opposite charged poles, earth is charged with magnetic, 'electrical' currents.

Using the Principles of Correspondence, which themselves entail polarity, the pagan perceiver understands that all manifestations of the ALL are carriers, receptor-transmitters, charged with current. All bodies, from the smallest particle to the largest galaxy, emit and hold charged or ionized bands.

A Catechism for the Children of De-Light

WHAT IS CHANGE?

Change is movement of polarity. 'Electrically' charged atoms undergoing 'electrolyte' disturbance convey identity to individual bodies. These pulsation's are sometimes electrical, sometimes more magnetic, always involving emissions of the continual life producing force, De-Light. Electrolyte change happens as a result of high temperatures, changes in radiation, intense frictional disturbance. Electrolyte-like changes happen in emotional states, thought patterning, or any life giving manifestation, because of the Principles of Correspondence, which allow us understanding of basic life-promoting processes.

In a mechanical sense what happens during electrolyte change is that electrons, or negative ions, are easily displaced. They are extremely fragile. Positive ions are weightier, we might say. A body in a positively charged ion atmosphere is functioning with an absence of electrons. A positively charged ion atmosphere is not conducive to well being or health. A proper balance must be maintained between negative ions and positive ions. An active electrical-magnetic field is more vital when there are slightly more of the fragile negative ions present.

Everyone has experienced the vitality of a waterfall or the atmosphere next to the oceans. Moving waters are filled with negative ions. They 'freshen' ion patterning in the air immediately around them. Preceding a storm air often becomes charged with positive ion energy. Animals lay down. Flies swarm and bite more than they had just a few hours before the change. Humans yawn and feel aches and pains more intensely. The air feels weighted. We feel drowsy. When the storm breaks, the rains make the air feel clean. Vitality is restored. The atmosphere regains its negative ion charge.

Everything that is in the totality of the ALL carries a positive and/or negative charge. Slippage back and forth, from prominence of one state to another, is what humans sense as change. When we identify the extremes of that slippage, we generate polarity. All beings, all living forms (minerals, waters, thoughts, signs, symbols, and words), ALL that is possible to understand is in vibratory, slippage motion—a tension state identifiable as oppositions, polarities. Nothing is without change.

One vibratory source of De-Light is different from another vibratory source of De-Light. We all emit the same life-giving energy, but each source is identifiable because of how it changes. Changes are constant. Emissions of De-Light speed up, slow down, constantly qualifying an identity. Whenever we appear to understand a life form, be it a person or plant, what we grasp is not, like a photograph of a moment locked in, but expressive of where that entity has moved. Moment-to-moment changes are usually not so radical as to disrupt understanding. If slippage occurs radically, making an identity more like its opposite than what it was, then we should attempt to understand that changed condition. What 'was' could well have transformed into something other. Change allows us to see that polarities themselves are only indications of a direction, a form, an understandable pattern; and those polarities indicate slippage toward other conditions. So death is not the end of life. It is an extreme indicator of slippage into another condition. Identification of polar opposites indicates movement or change.

Cataclysmic change is feared by humans. Yet it happens all the time. Volcanoes erupt. Suns nova. Tornadoes and earthquakes shake apart human constructions. People in one form of relationship, marriage for example, suddenly enter another form of relationship, divorce. Calm domesticated dogs suddenly become killers. When conditions of polarity overtake what appears as non-change or very slow change (slippage) the drama excites and threatens us. Cataclysmic change seems overpowering because it indicates we have become comfortable with a condition, a polarity. Change is discomforting when it is extreme. It is an indicator of how pervasive is De-Light, continual creating.

SHOULD WE MONITOR SLIPPAGES AND CATACLYSMS?

Pagan consciousness places great emphasis on measuring apparent constancy of relationships and on apparent disruptions of that constancy. Much of what we know of the world's great cultures consists of devices for measuring relationships large and small, of Earth and Sun and Moon, of frogs, fish runs and birds mating. Transformation change is the essence of all story-teachings from all cultures.

Some changes are constant. The Sun imparts a daily rhythm on terrestrial magnetic currents. As our planet is tilted toward or away from the Sun the flow of the life-generating solar forces is either stronger or weaker. Earth beings experience this change as the difference between hot and cold, Summer and Winter. This seasonal pattern of change affects the emanations or radiations of all earth beings. Birds migrate, as do Elk, Bears, and Butterflies, in synchronization with the seasonal shifting of polarities. Bacteria and other living soil creatures bring about fertility within narrow temperature zones in consort with how seasons change in various locations. All biological activity slows when it is too cold. Too much heat has a similar effect. Should major disruption to these seasonal changes between polarities occur, normal life would likely be disrupted. For instance, if several major volcanoes spewed dust into the air, forming a cloud over major portions of the earth, the Sun's warming would be blocked. Fertility would be diminished. The abundance of food would diminish. Migrations, female and male fertility cycles, all kinds of normal or predictable cycles might be changed. Human memory of such cataclysmic events remains with us and reminds us that all is temporary, that contingencies must be allowed for. Because of correspondence, these earth events suggest that as humans we are wise to pay attention to cosmic changes of similar explosive magnitude. Solar flares, eclipses, the proximity of planets to each other, asteroids on course for collision, all could disrupt patterns which humans and other species have adjusted to over time.

Subtle changes, such as the lunar cycle affect all earth life. Ocean tides are visible as a result. Terrestrial magnetic flow changes are not visible but are every bit as intense as ocean tides. During a full moon there is an increase in magnetic activity around noon, with a quiet period just before sunrise. Eclipses of the moon have no apparent physical effect upon the Earth and its creatures, but they do change the level of terrestrial magnetism, a subtle disruption of normal patterns, apparently triggering volcanic eruptions and earthquakes. Charged currents are in continual flux. The relationship of polarities is never constant. Solar flare-ups or storms are known to change the flow of charged particles, severely disturbing the magnetic equilibrium. These magnetic storms don't just affect great bodies like planets. Such storms cause disruptions and realignments in the force fields of all entities, including elemental metals, physical forms, and mental-spiritual phenomena.

Each entity exists in a state of tension-vibration. Its interactions with other entities affects the quality of that vibrational tension. The relative polarity of any two entities describe conditions of stability or possible extreme shifting.

Magnetic realignments effectively change the nature of the relationship of any polarities. In 'storm' conditions positive can become negative, negative can disappear, or negative charges might appear in greater quantities.

Monitoring these changes and moving with them is a great part of the human lesson. When we live as though continual magnetic change is not happening, pretending that life is a 'steady state', the consequences can be deadly for humans and all other beings. This is especially true during a time when with our technologies we pretend to manage the planet and the Life Force itself.

The magnetic nature of poles means that a current or Force, which is attracted by one pole, will be repelled by the other. Because of this Positive and Negative electrical charge characteristic, poles are seen as opposites. This principle, through correspondence, exists throughout all life. Attraction and repulsion is the universal dance. Being aware, while immersed in this dance, is how we come into an understanding of daily, momentary, De-Light (filled) experiences.

WHAT IS DUALISM?

How we talk about polarities betrays our understanding of continual change, of continual creation, of De-Light manifesting into and throughout life. It is very easy to begin talking as if one pole has more value than its opposite. We do this all the time, particularly in Westernized civilizations, and especially where the dominant culture shapes language. When apparent opposites are seen as two paired entities that are fundamentally not alike, then differences rather than similarities are emphasized. The circular image representing the ALL is split.

Splitting, or dividing-into-two, stops motion. Rigid distinctions, eventually protected as truths, determine how we think, see, talk, give value. In this situation, continual creation, De-Light is rarely present. When De-Light is recognized, it is placed within a polarity context, and is often feared, seen as evil, dismissed as wild, untamed, ungraspable.

Dualism is the result of rigidifying apparent polarities. Even though many ancient records reveal the primary role of vibration and continual creative motion as the essence of the ALL, many other records codify division. Doctrines of division between Spirit and Matter written by ancient Greeks, Egyptians, Persians, and both Amerindians and Oriental 'Indians,' show that many languages have rigid or dualistic understandings of polarity. This dualism exists in our time as the primary thought and language form of the dominant culture. International corporate culture and the religious orthodoxies maintain their power through the basic language constructions that maintain rigid distinctions between what appear as polar opposites. Management of what is wild, continually changing, De-Light(ful), is the primary task of the dominant culture.

A Catechism for the Children of De-Light

There are occasions, in a remote, carefully illustrated, historic past, when De-Light broke through the dualism, when 'magic' happened, when manifestations of the ALL in a hierarchical sense (the necessary support of one part of duality; God as Father) are allowed. For Christians this unification took place in the life of Jesus the Christ. For Islamic practitioners the life of Mohammed effectively bridged the rigid dualism. Other 'saints' show elements of similar magical attainments, but these awarenesses are understood as set aside, outside of the 'normal' and thus not possible for the masses of humans or for any other life forms to attain. The dominant culture, in support of its orthodox conceptions, makes use of language devices— world pictures—that are either black or white, evil or good. One side of this dualistic reality is codified into what is good, right, expected. If a person is not practicing what lies within this set of laws, then that person is damned, persecuted, because in the eyes of the dominant culture they practice the work, in varying forms, of the Devil.

Dualism within language allows for power in relationships. When value is given to one side as opposed to a perceived opposition, that practice sets the conditions for accepting institutions and war. Institutions are rigidified forms in human societies based on perpetuating one side of a perceived duality.

All institutions derive their legitimacy from the linguistic habit of speaking as if dualities exist. Pick any institution as a test: Marriage, Universities, Churches-Temples, Mosques, Senates, Corporations and many others. The dominant culture promotes institutions because the very establishment of any institution rigidifies, manages, controls De-LIGHT. Conforming 'life'—lived in agreement with the dualistic realities—is rewarded with what is placed on the valued side of an entire list of dualities: Heaven, Riches, you can name more.

The dominant civilizing forces have for several thousand years promoted human dualism as reality. What we tend to find interesting, exciting, is the play between polarized categories. In this worldview all relationship is competitive and potentially combative. Our stories are dramas laying out various human warfares. In our stories some categories are simply Right, others are Wrong. Some are High, others are Low. Judgment and correct choice are required if one is to receive rewards rather than hardships. We are entertained by watching combative relationships. All our sports, all our 'shows' follow this format. A very minimal list of the typical polarities that command our interest follows. You can think of many more that show our dualistic habit.

Work - Pleasure	Faith - Disloyal	Trust - Betrayal
Love - Hate	Scientific - Folk	Popular - Artistic
Community - Alone	Individual - Conformist	

By using dualism as habit in our language, we tend to act in terms of that habit. Words and conceptions are primary in all forms of human management.

Words given value—repeated and rewarded—effectively control human behavior in accord with the management goals of the dominant culture. That this control is seen as a sickness or the root of most suffering by practitioners of De-Light, is (1) threatening, and (2) not even comprehensible, by managers within the dominant culture.

In the dominant culture a primary distinction is always made between the rational and the emotional (or spiritual). Any language habit that does not reflect dualism as the norm is rejected as irrational. Vibrational feelings and other sensory languages are suspect, laughable. With the dualistic viewpoint, most of life, i.e. continual creation, is rejected or not considered as relevant. Whole realms of De-Light are not even considered, because they do not reflect the dualism, and are therefore not manageable.

DOES EVERYONE ACCEPT DUALISM?

Dualism is not the language of De-Light. Nonetheless, those who understand continual creativity, since they exist in the linguistic framework of, and must attempt to communicate with, the dominant language, face the challenge of conveying their meaning. Expressing their meaning, with a language that inherently creates a false duality, takes skill to use that language and to transcend that limiting language at the same time.

William Blake (as have many artists and philosophers) struggled to go beyond the dualism implied in our languages. Blake, in *THE MARRIAGE OF HEAVEN AND HELL,* introduces the notion of *Contraries*:

> "Without Contraries is no progression. Attraction and Repulsion, Reasons and Energy, Love and Hate, are necessary to Human existence! From these contraries spring what the religious call Good & Evil. Good is the passive that obeys Reason. Evil is the active springing from Energy. Good is Heaven. Evil is Hell."

Later he has the voice of the Devil say:

> "1. Man has no Body distinct from his Soul; for that called Body is a portion of Soul discerned by the five Senses, the chief inlets of Soul in this age. 2. Energy is the only life, and is from the Body; and Reason is the bound or outward circumference of Energy. 3. Energy is Eternal Delight."

Blake understood that the entrenched dualism of the West, held sacred by the Church, Mosque, Temple complex, was joyless. The splitting of polarities stops the natural interplay of the magnetic energies. Dualism is Rational Death. Pagans of all times preferred a Joyful Wisdom, human lives filled with fascination and discovery.

IS THERE ANY WAY TO KEEP FROM FALLING INTO THE DUALISTIC TRAP?

Remember that whatever we isolate as extremes, polarities, opposites, is the result of continual motion, creative action, De-Light. We can gain further insight into this most basic 'pagan' awareness when we look at charged energies in their contextual environment.

If there exists a relationship (at least two unlike entities or identifiable sources of energy) then what transpires as the quantity and quality of the energy of that relationship will depend upon the 'atmosphere' within which that relationship takes place. For instance, if a man and a woman (positive and negative polarity) are in Love, and if the community which surrounds them is charged with Love, then their energy-charges find support. If that surrounding community is full of Fear energy, then their Love is continually compromised. In some cases their Love energy could be seen as a threat. Then Love, rather than sharing, becomes conflict. (The basis for stories like Romeo and Juliet).

Similarly, if we look at polarities such as Feasting and Fasting in the contexts of Famine or Abundance, the relationship of those polarities changes, depending upon the greater context in which they are found.

In extreme cases of contextual energy exchange we can observe what is called Transmutation. One energy-entity is so overpowered by the other that it becomes the other. It is usually understood that only like kinds of energies can be transmuted. Love can become Hate under certain conditions, Hot can become Cold, Courage may become Fear.

There is the possibility, however, in severe overpowering situations that entities and energies that are unlike each other can transmute. Love can become Fear. Feasting can become Famine. Given the proper contexts of energy, Humans can become Animals. Horses can become Birds. Plants can become Beams of Light. All is possible when energy entities are charged in a particular magnetic field. These transmutations are generally understood as magical.

Usually those who do not believe in Duality, but do recognize the prominence of Polarity in all things, speak of polar relationships as 'a Matter of degree.' Let us use Love as an example again. Love is usually given a positive charge, and is associated with Good and Right. Hate is given a negative change and is associated with Bad and Wrong. To bridge the implied duality, we say that Love is more positive and less negative. On a shaded scale, Hate is always present in Love, and Love is always present in Hate. But it is a matter of degree as to where Love and Hate separate.

What is usually stated when discussions of degree are entertained is that "there is a natural tendency in the direction of the dominance of the Positive Pole." Of course the Positive Pole is associated with, culturally skewed toward, the Male vibrational energy. The perception supporting a direction of dominance, an emphasis toward a pole of primary energy, is a choice of value. It is subtle, but it indicates that any energy choice exists in masked form behind the discussion of degree. That choice has in fact split the polarity into a duality.

Another way of stating the degree concept is in terms of color metaphor. The polarities are set on a scale reflecting the primary colors of the prism, ranging from red to violet with orange, yellow, green, indigo and blue in-between.

There is another way that we can understand that extremes are dangerous. Think of a thermometer. Polarities of Hot and Cold are measured there. If we look at that thermometer in terms of Life and Death, then we can easily see that too much Heat or too much Cold is Anti-Life. The temperate zones in the middle are the best for most life.

In the thermometer example we can also see the contextual relativity of polarities. Hot is often equated with Hell and Evil and Bad in the dominant culture. Cold could just as easily be Evil or Bad in its extreme, which is also anti-life.

There exists a concept in many cultures, which may get beyond duality and beyond the notion of the tendency of energy to flow toward the Positive Pole. That is the concept of Mirroring or Reflection. Mirroring is often understood in terms of the Tree of Life. This tree is prominent in the Sun dance cultures of the American Indians of the plains, as it is in African cultures. It may have been an understanding among the Essene sect of the Judaic culture. In symbolic form the Tree is forked, above and below the ground.

The leaves of this tree are symbolically made of mirrors. The limbs are understood as polarities. The trunk carries the life force from the leaves to the Oneness of rooting in Earth. Likewise the trunk carries the life force of earth into the limbs and branches and into the mirroring itself. The same winds blow all the leaves (mirrors). Leaves do not necessarily mirror what is commonly understood as a polar opposition. Depending upon where the Sun dancer is moving in relation to the mirroring leaves, the mirroring is ever and always changing. From some positions certain leaves might appear to be reflecting commonly held oppositions, polarities, or contraries. Love might be reflecting Hate. Joy might be reflecting Sorrow. Hot/Cold. Fear/Courage. But within the Sun dance, which is symbolic of our daily dance within the ALL, a dancer's movements might be such that Joy begins reflecting Fear. Another move might put one's energy focus on one limb of the reflecting tree. Whole new polarities might appear. Love might be in contrary relationship with Joy. Courage might be in polarity with Bravery.

What is implied is that there exists Polarity, there exists a positive and negative charge, but that any entity of energy carries both these charges. It depends upon contextual and/or focused perceiving energy as to how that polarity is manifested.

One other interesting element in this Sun dance way of understanding polarities is that it deals with the notion of Positive or Male dominance. The most visual parts of the tree thrust upward and are understood as positively charged. But the invisible parts of the tree, the rooting, are considered primary to the life possibility of that tree. Vibrational energies within the soil feed the thrusting. Solar vibrational energies also feed that upward motion. But it would do no good to have the Positive Pole if there were no rooted, feminine, Negative Pole. The effect, it is said, would be like a drummer beating upon a drum without a skin. The life force, De-Light, requires a proper balancing of the positive and negative polarities for continual creation to happen.

Awareness in decision-making based on Part IV

1. Motion never stops.
2. Change happens every moment.
3. Monitoring or measuring change gives us direction.
4. Rigidities of any kind eventually crumble.
5. Opposites, seen as duality, mirror.

PART V
PRINCIPLES OF
RHYTHM - MEASURE

"Keeping time, time time, In a sort of Runic rhyme, To the tintinnabulation that so musically wells From the bells, bells, bells, bells, Bells, bells, bells."
— Edgar Allan Poe —

A Catechism for the Children of De-Light

WHAT IS RHYTHM?

Bells, Bells, Bells. The energies of De-Light most easily manifest into human reality through measure, repetition. Rhythm is sensual. Often rhythmic acts are not conscious. Breathing, in-out, in-out, our most basic rhythmic action happens several times a minute without us taking notice. Minutes happen, hours, weeks, years; we may think to celebrate events in their passing, but the rhythmic flow filling our lives with meaning is usually not in the center of our attention.

Rhythm is a sensation repeated. It can be a sound, a touch, an image, a smell, a motion. The process of that sensation happening over and over becomes part of an individual's story, our truths, our realities.

HOW DOES RHYTHM AFFECT US?

Rhythm works at primary cellular levels to affect the patterning of all life. All manifestations into physical reality reveal adherence to principles of polarity (Part IV). Between poles there is continual motion. As this motion is encountered by all human sensitivities, likeness, similarity, is sensed. The experience of a creeping sensation over and over excites our cells. Rhythmic sensation usually effervesces, lifts, makes us feel outpouring life. Our heartbeats are rhythmic De-Light within this material plane of being.

Even severing the motion between polarities, what we perceive as Death, is itself a polarity exhibiting creative motion, which often becomes rhythmic.

What goes one way will go the other. Even the most subtle, invisible wave energies can be interrupted or broken, but they will find completion, over and over again.

How long an atom, object, entity or emotion spends at a particular pole is in contrast to how long it spends at the opposite pole. As it returns to the first pole and begins the cycle over, a periodicity is established. Recurrence, the repetition of the motion at regular intervals, establishes a rhythm.

A Catechism for the Children of De-Light

How long a particular cycle takes to complete itself or some part of itself is its measure. Measure is the extent or limit, the range or dimension of rhythm.

We often take rhythms for granted. Rhythmic sensations are experienced as what we expect, what is normal. Rhythmic repetition comforts us, gives us a sense of security. Within the flow of life's rhythms it is the unexpected that jolts us. If a season ends and the sun does not appear, breathing becomes irregular, a woman's moon time varies, our lives are suddenly disrupted. Our experience of creative De-Light requires the steady drum, the heartbeats that are the bells, bells, bells, of ongoing life.

WHY IS RHYTHM SO IMPORTANT?

Natural rhythms set up human habits. If we live in a climate where two seasons dominate, we walk, work, talk and celebrate differently than we do if four seasons are distinctly dominant. Natural rhythms, coming and going, have a primary influence on human choice. We make decisions based on how manifestations of natural rhythms feel.

It is very important to be aware of this relationship of natural rhythms and habit. Human communities, having related in certain ways to all pervading rhythms, have created and culturally instilled various habitual behaviors. If those rhythms change, as a result of human dominance over this world's processes, then we are in effect dancing to another drumbeat, or subtly changed drumbeat. Coordinating our choices to this different beat, may be difficult, because of habitual ways of dealing with a pervading rhythm. What does it take to change dance steps?

HOW CAN RHYTHM BE USED?

Rhythm is primal. Sensations of rhythm open us primally. We each know this, but are usually not aware of the power of rhythms in our lives. To appreciate our susceptibility, consider what recurrent touching during lovemaking feels like, how these rhythms can release us, get us to let go, experience the flow of creative De-Light. Or consider how recurrent smells of a certain woman or man can overpower all our defenses, give us comfort, desire, longing and a host of raw, primal emotions. The quiet of a forest with songs of birds in their rhythms can allow us a similar primal opening, as can waves washing in and out along the shore. Natural rhythm allows us to attune to all that is, to all polarities, to all creative motion.

So what happens when humans change the beat? What is the relationship between rhythm and intention? Human cultures are formed of rhythmic interpretation. The interpreters (priests or priestesses) know that rhythm patterns become human habit, and that habit is a key factor in human choice, decision, how we live with our world.

So, if these priests or priestesses can establish human rhythmic interpretations utilizing rhythmic sensual tools of sound, touch, smell, image, then it is possible that their peculiar human interpretations of natural rhythms can become as powerful as natural rhythms themselves, can direct human and planetary destiny.

This is how humans agree on culture. Culture(s) prevail as decision-making mediums because each has formulated sensual rhythms that have become habit, habit as strong as those based on raw or primal rhythms. Cultures are masks which humans live out as realities.

Human cultures are always noisy, rhythmically. Songs, music of all kinds, chanting, drumming are keys to opening human primal awareness of rhythm and overpowering it with a direction of interpretation. Bells ringing on the hour, clocks ticking, a voice calling across the village for prayers, all human measurements are interventions within the natural flow of rhythms with human rhythms. We are controlled very subtly by our rhythmic agreements with whatever is the dominant culture.

Because rhythms are so primly powerful, even the human version of dominant rhythms nudges an individual toward a merging. Rhythms carry us beyond ourselves. They are the key to shedding individuality. Feel it as you dance, as you sing in a choir or by yourself on a mountain top, as you make love. Rhythms are what carry us most easily into the sensation of cosmic De-Light. And for that very reason they can be subtly dangerous, for they can be the manipulations of interpreters who would direct our merging.

The dominant culture of our sub-Aquarius time reinforces rhythms of speed. Electronic music of all kinds, communication linkages that utilize wave energies to allow for instantaneous gratification, time patterns governed by work security within and supportive of dominant economic interpretations, all these interventions block or diminish the impact of natural rhythms. When natural rhythms blast through, causing a cataclysm that disrupts human rhythm patterning, then we try to second-guess those natural rhythms, see the periodicity of earthquakes, tropical storms, floods, pestilence. We can't prevent natural rhythmic outpourings. But we can assess their effects.

For pagans a more important job is assessing the effects of dominant culture rhythm making on all life with a goal of diminishing those effects.

WHAT IS THE NATURE OF RHYTHMIC PATTERNING?

The nature of rhythmic patterning and change is most easily discussed using musical terminology. The heartbeat or life-force drum is the primary vehicle through which we feel creative De-Light. Its sound is steady, speeding up or slowing down depending upon the context in which it is found.

A 26,000-year cycle is large enough that the rhythms going into it are rather plodding in nature (Recall the prior discussion of elliptical orbits and 'precession of the equinoxes' or the 'great year.') By comparison, a cycle of yearly birthdays, is very rapid; and a cycle of one day is very, very fast paced.

Some rhythms hangout around one element of a polarity longer than they do around the opposite polarity. This leads to a kind of syncopated pattern, which human music mimics.

Some rhythms are very free-flowing like an uninterrupted stream. These patterns have what we call a romantic or lyric quality as opposed to rhythms which are more staccato. Humans' rhythms reflect natural rhythms, even when they are chosen as counterpoint to natural rhythms.

Human awareness is what makes our species unique. Our psychological selves, reflecting the physical rhythmic world, are cyclic, manifest rhythmically.

Patterns of conscious to unconscious behavior are rhythmic, predictable, measurable. Focusing attention energy moves us toward conscious or unconscious behavior. We seem to know what we are doing, we are not just doing.

What is important here is to understand that with attention-energy we can intercept consciousness-unconsciousness, and we can redirect the given rhythmic pattern. We do this all the time, unconsciously. These acts of interruption can become habitual themselves, causing us to feel like we are stumbling through reality, caught by consciousness triggers. Thoughts, images, the stuff of mental rhythms, can make us feel trapped, unable to let go and feel the cosmic stream of De-Light flowing forth.

DO RHYTHMS SET OUR DESTINY?

Larger rhythmic cycles are energies being emitted. Earth, all the planets, solar systems, galaxies are all emitting rhythmic energy. Those rhythmic patterns are how we humans recognize where we are and what we are. Measurements of these greater emissive forces tell us (especially whoever is the prevailing priesthood; in our day the scientists) how these rhythms will play out over time. But priests interpret within their peculiar frameworks. So for scientists the apparent demise of the sun in 5 billion years is a valuable interpretation which determines the temporary nature of all Earth life. For a pagan, seeing those same cycles, may be an affirmation that all life energy is continually creating itself, that we are manifest in this form momentarily, that the energies that are us may manifest in other ways in other universes, possibly even as we move through this apparent moment, simultaneously. In this sense our creative manifestations are gambles within apparent prevailing energy currents. Probable realities are everywhere.

Are we on a merry-go-round from which we can't escape? Or a revolving wheel which determines our fates, life after life? Possibly, but only because we agree to interpret rhythms that way. Using attention-energy we are capable of transmuting any element of any energy pattern, of dancing differently to any rhythm. We can interrupt rhythms, redirect them, and in so doing we do not have to leave behind any natural rhythmic pattern. How we merge and incorporate our dance with the cosmic dance is what makes life De-Lightful.

As energy dancers we do not escape polarity, nor do we leave cyclic rhythm behind. We learn to appreciate the always-present vibration-energy music. We learn to follow or create steps, which are pleasant within those rhythms.

The Hermetists speak of the Law of Compensation. This law is understood in that everyone 'pays the price' of anything which is possessed or needed. The millionaire will pay in sickness and sorrow through many lives for the manipulations of energy which brought him material gain. The poor peasant will gain in song and merriment a joy that no rich man can know in this life.

What this Law of Compensation is addressing is what we have termed the interruptive aspect of a cycle or rhythmic pattern. Introducing a human rhythmic choice, through focusing the attention-energy of that choice, carries with it predictable consequences. Decision-making not only involves choice, it involves what is not chosen. What is not chosen may go unseen and unfelt during one lifetime. But when the life cycle is repeated, the unchosen interruption will likely have cycled forth itself.

The millionaire will therefore experience poverty, of necessity, because this completes the rhythmic cycling of energy. The healthy will experience sickness. Those who poison for gain will be poisoned and will suffer loss.

Interruptive patterns can be introduced again; the cyclic energies can be further complicated. Compensation or Karma can be postponed. But what goes around comes around. The measure of life is rhythm, no matter how many layers of rhythm, all happening simultaneously, in the eternal moment as well as over time.

Awareness in decision-making based on Part V

1. Energies repeat.
2. Habits allow continuity.
3. Our intention can change the beat.
4. We dance cosmically.

PART VI
PRINCIPLES OF CAUSE
AND SYNCHRONICITY

"Every cause produces more than one effect."
— Herbert Spencer —

A Catechism for the Children of De-Light

WHAT IS THE BEGINNING?

When we accept the orderliness of the ALL (refer to Part I) we cannot imagine existence without precedence. There is always 'that which came before.' The Creator precedes Creation in order, rank and time.

From the pagan perspective of continual, delightful creation welling-up into all life is a beginning implied? Is there necessarily a source for continual life-giving energy? It is very difficult to conceive of process not coming from somewhere. But perhaps that is a problem with conceptualization. Perhaps thinking about rather than experiencing limits what we 'know.' Perhaps continual De-Light just is, ever outpouring, ever being, never ending and never beginning.

There are many ways of designing order as we conceive of our universe. Each involves limits. Each implies a beginning from which all else follows.

Most often our languages are set up to imply that Cause is an active polarity producing Effect. Reality moves in a direction. That causal connective presupposes concepts of fixed Space and Time. When we say that something 'caused' something else, our mental framework can usually be accurately portrayed by picturing an object bumping into another object. Bodies in motion, be they atoms or planets, bump, pull, smash, transform. This causes the universe to be the way it is. A corollary of this picture is the Creation image where a Father or Mother figure releases (causes) life, bringing about the worlds we know.

A sophisticated discussion of Cause details these bodies as events. It is understood that "one event makes possible another event." Chains of events, moving in a direction, appear as progress. Again these events are anchored in a conception of Space (three-dimensional) and Time (usually linear). Sacred events, those celebrated in holy books, move the event into four dimensions of Space, one non-material (or spiritual). This movement opens up time so that a sacred event can continue, through ritual, liturgy, celebration.

IS CAUSE OUR ONLY BASIC ORDERING PRINCIPLE?

Pagan consciousness does not always see in terms of an event being a link in a preceding orderly chain. Cause is not the only ordering principle. If Space and Time are themselves flowing, open—De-Light-filled energies, non-linear in nature—then the notion of Cause as a primary connective, as what makes order or sense of a jumbled universe, falls away. Cause then only has a partial relevance. For pagans, simultaneity is at least as major a connective as cause. Simultaneity of events across dimensions of material and non-material reality just happens. Those events themselves may become causes for whole chains of consequences and can therefore be investigated, discovered, unraveled. But the apparent original events or Causes may be accidental, chance, the results of energy attractions that are/were probable but not necessarily possible.

Along the same lines of understanding, the psychologist Carl G. Jung wrote of yet another connecting principle which he saw functioning in many pagan cultures. He named it Synchronicity. Synchronicity refers to a connection in the specific situation where two events happen simultaneously and are clearly causally unrelated. The effect of such Synchronicity is meaningful.

WHY ARE OUR LANGUAGES SO DEPENDENT ON CAUSAL CONNECTIVES?

We speak, think, use language(s) to establish order in our world. Without connectives there seems to be nothing that creates order and attains meaning. If we have two unrelated events, such as a tree standing in a woods and a stone sitting along the edge of a stream, there is no reason to consider a linkage between those two events in any given moment. But, if the rock were suddenly to strike the tree, causing it to bleed, become weak, and susceptible to disease, then an event has occurred which is charged with meaning. Or a little old lady might be stumbling along a sidewalk after having cashed her pension check at the bank. Her motion in crossing a busy street might cause a traffic jam and lots of angry people honking their horns. But what gives meaning to this particular afternoon drama is the thief who jumps from the shadows of a doorway, knocks her down, steals her purse and money. He causes the little old lady to become a victim, an injured person in an ambulance, and a person with no money to pay for rent and food.

All events derive meaning as we discover their causes. Some events are more highly charged than other events. These are said to be more meaningful.

The meaningfulness of events, the relative importance of cause, distinguishes individuals from each other. It also makes (causes) one culture to differ from another. Cultures are agreements of how we interpret events. Events relating to the patriarchs before Moses are charged with meaning for the Church, Mosque and Temple orthodoxy. The Crucifixion of Christ and his Resurrection are events which contain the whole reason for the existence of Christianity. Similarly, Mohammed's life is charged with meaning and is the 'cause' behind Islam. When these charged causal relationships are anointed with divinity, they take on the status of primary causes for those who believe in them. Belief in primary causal events orders how we humans live. This gives comfort. Belief in primary casual events removes primal unknowing, likely affecting the experience of fear.

If the primal causal event is felt as ongoing—manifest in every moment as a continually effervescent Delightful energy—a continual alertness is required. There are no excuses. There is no his/her story on which to depend, on which to establish forgiveness for actions or inactions. There is only 'now,' this moment, how you interact most fully in it with all options a possibility, with all choices happening simultaneously. If our languages were changed to reveal such continual creation, human life would be very different. Human awareness would move beyond linear polarity. A simultaneous beginning of all life would replace causal connectives. Song would most likely replace talk.

WHAT ARE PROBLEMS?

Cause-Effect ordering, as our principle mode of understanding how we operate within our world, generates 'problems.' Problems of Free Will within Determinism come from thinking like a plumber who deals with non-flowing water within a plumbing system. Problems, be they mathematical, physical, philosophical, religious, or simply mechanical, imply solutions. Solutions in turn imply a situation or set of events—a purified state—against which we measure our corrective actions because we believe this state or goal constitutes what 'should be.' Problems allow human will to generate solutions. As modern humans, most of our time is spent in interaction with languages of problems. Why? Because we accept definitions of reality that are causal and usually linear; we assume stasis, a fixed state, to which all variants should and can return.

Problem solving or gaming (overcoming opposition which is problematic) keeps humans talking and acting within narrow, causal frameworks. The energies associated with causally linked meaning (problem solving) are repetitive rhythms, overpowering enough to form neat worlds that cannot be easily penetrated by energies that are non-causal. A primary difference between pagan cultures and modern dominant cultures is that pagan cultures are set up to stimulate energies that are non-causal. Different realities are lived. Problems are not solved. Resolution may appear to happen within the creative process of an event, but it is understood that such resolution is itself only momentary, is only a probable illusion.

The dominant culture relishes-in alertness to problems. Power over the masses of peoples is maintained by constant bombardment through 'news' of all our problems. We spend most of our energies as humans in solutions, whether they be wars, public works programs, programs of welfare, programs for the ultimate in education (which teaches proper problem solving). The net affect of all this energy focused on human problems is that individuals are weighed down with the overwhelming complexity and thus the impossibility of being anything other than dependent upon various problem solvers or power structures. A great deal of effort goes into keeping the mass culture fragmented and thus merely pieces, or possibly players, in problem solving power games.

If a person, for whatever reason, moves beyond living exclusively within the confines of causal reality, then that person ceases to be a piece or a player in the human power game. Once we suddenly understand that causally based languages keep us enslaved, once we see that environments, opinions, thoughts, customs shaped by these languages limit our very beings, then we have an opportunity to begin breaking away. We know or sense why we do what we do. The process of this discovery is the pathway of Mastery.

Directing one's life does not mean control over cause-effect linkages, nor does it mean control over or even confrontation with problem solving power centers, be they religious and educational institutions, corporations or governments. Taking control or moving outside the causal reality means directing   the interferences that penetrate the primary life force energies. It means opening to De-Light. In effect, the person who establishes mastery of direction for his or her own life sets up a switch which cycles current differently. The dominant culture goes on. But its controlling interferences are not able to overpower creative energies. A master player in a causal game is free to set the direction of that game, its duration, the experiences within that game. That mastery may allow other non-causal energies to be experienced.

Mastery, for pagans, comes through experience. As one becomes the hunter rather than the hunted, the mechanic rather than one who needs fixing, the healer rather than the victim of sickness, the farmer rather than one who eats, one becomes more than the processes in which s/he evolves. By allowing the totality of energy events within one's experience, all life, moment to moment is a teaching, is sacred. There is no need for instituting sacredness, no need for Churches, Mosques, Temples, seats of government, palaces, etc.

A Catechism for the Children of De-Light

Two stories from my experience might help in understanding the relationship between causally linked realties and meaningful events that are non-causal in nature.

One week I had been hired to work with the Forest Service in gathering information and making a determination about the fate of a mountain. A group of Forest Service officials and outside consultants spent two days interviewing people who had lived for many years in the area. Some were there because of the timber resources. Because the Mountain had been 'sacred' to the native Indian people, they were involved in discussions.

On the evening of the third day the group loaded canoes at the West edge of the lake and paddled to a Fisheries Camp some miles up the lake. There we cooked our evening meal and started a roaring campfire. Around the campfire a discussion of what had been learned from all those who were interviewed took place. A Native American friend and I felt moved to go away from the circle. We didn't want to appear impolite, so we sat outside the campfire circle, away from the vibrations of the discussion. The head forester of the National Forest had also been moved to leave the fire circle. At the time we didn't know that the head forester was a few feet behind where we sat propped against two trees.

The act of stepping quietly aside allowed the energies of the whole scene to transform. First a snow-white owl swooped down from the South over the men around the fire and took up a perch in the North. The men around the fire were not aware of the owl's flight. Then from the direction of the Mountain, in the North and West from our position, three Great Horned owls came toward us. One took up a position in the West, one flew to the East of us, and the other landed on a limb to the South. Once they had established their positions they began 'talking.'

It was clear to me, and I felt it was clear to my Indian friend, that the owls had come to council with us about the mountain. I looked at my friend and whispered "what are they saying." He said that they were saying "NO" in the language of his people. I knew instantly that they were there to make a plea for the future of the Mountain.

A Catechism for the Children of De-Light

The head forester had observed the scene. He saw the men around the fire, talking, rather loudly, on and on. He saw the owls come. He felt our communicative link with the owls. He saw us share our understanding. He felt our recognition sent silently to the owls. He saw them simultaneously fly from their perches, all heading toward the Mountain. He came up behind us and whispered, "what did they say?"

We told him that the owls had come to council. That they had communicated "NO," that the mountain was not to be developed. Condos and a ski run were in the development plans. He nodded as we spoke. Then he went to the men around the fire. He interrupted their loud discussion and quietly told them that an event had just happened, that they had been in the middle of the event, but that they had not experienced it. He told them that he wanted them to know what had happened. Then he had me tell them about the owls. Their faces told me that they considered such information extraneous and beyond belief.

The next morning, at dawn, the head forester and I pushed off in a canoe out into the lake which mirrored all the colors of sunrise. The others slept. We had paddled awhile when my attention was directed to an Osprey sitting almost overhead on an old snag, watching us. I felt the bird wondering about what was going to happen to the mountain. I asked the head forester if he had made a decision. He turned from his place in the front of the canoe and with a sparkle in his eyes he said, "the owls decided." The Osprey heard those words and flew off, in the direction of the mountain.

There are many Causal links in what has become a story charged with meaning for myself and for many others. Twenty years later that mountain has again come under pressure from those in power. There is a different head forester. But the decisions made as a result of our communion with the owls stand. The situation of the story does not submit to causal analysis. The event of the owls happened simultaneously with the event of the campfire. The two events are causally unrelated. Four owls sitting around in the trees has nothing to do with a discussion about the fate of a mountain. Yet, for three humans, stepping outside, moving within our potential for human mastery, these two events had a profound connectedness. That connectedness and our sensitivity to it saved a mountain from human development.

Carl Jung describes Synchronicity as that connecting principle in the following way:

> "In all these cases and others like them there seems to be an *a priori*, causally inexplicable knowledge of a situation which at the time is unknowable. Synchronicity therefore consists of two factors: a) An unconscious image comes into consciousness either in the form of a dream, idea, or premonition. b) An objective situation coincides with this content. The one is as puzzling as the other. How does the unconscious image arise, and how the coincidence? I understand only to well why people prefer to doubt the reality of these things."
>
> — *Synchronicity: An Acausal Connecting Principle Collected Work* - Vol. 8: page 447 —

Some might relegate such a Synchronistic event to the realms of the psycho-physical. This would mean that Synchronicity was not a true connecting principle, as basic as Cause to our understanding of how the universe works. A psycho-physical event requires human participation. Without my Indian friend and myself the event would not have taken place. True or untrue? It is true that the foresters may never have learned of the event of the owls if we hadn't recognized it. But the fact of the owl's participation in the discussions surrounding the Mountain would have taken place without our recognition. The owls 'knew' of their participation. So there was 'recognition' by them whether or not humans participated. How they knew requires that we move beyond causality. Among pagan people major and minor decisions often include for consideration what information is available within causal reality, then wait for other sorts of events to inform—universal patterning in other than causal reflections.

A second experience illustrates the a-causal connective at work in another way.

For some time I had been given a strong sense that I was to finish all of my custom rototilling and mowing by a certain date. When the date arrived, I wasn't finished. There was one job left. So I loaded the tractor onto a trailer and headed toward the job. I was tense, knowing that I was supposed to have finished, but not knowing why. On the way to the job a tire blew out on the trailer. This, in all my years of work, had never happened. Fortunately I was near a tire shop and got it fixed without too much trouble. But it cost all that was to be made by doing the mowing job. During the job, there was a loud mechanical clatter. I turned off the mower and noticed that parts had begun vibrating off from the machine. I fixed this. Then it happened a second time, just as I was finishing the job. While lying on my back fixing the machine again, a formation of Crows swooped low across the yard, in front of my vision. In that instant I remembered a dream in which I was laying on my back and the same group of Crows had swooped past. In the dream the Crows were a sign that a group of people were waiting for me to show up to teach them.

I finished the job having made no money, loaded the tractor, and headed home. When I drove in the driveway, under a tree on the lawn was a large group of people, only one of whom I'd ever seen before. They were waiting for me to talk with them.

The premonition about timing did not cause the tractor to break down. Nor did it cause the flat tire. But there was a definite relationship between what I had been 'told to do,' the crows and the crowd. This complex scenario is typical of how life seems to unfold once the limitations of causality become only part of how we interpret what is going on. Simultaneous, unrelated events in space and time all add up to meaning. We live in that kind of complexity surrounding us daily. The pagan person is likely to be acutely aware of levels of meaning that are missed by those who accept causality as the only connecting principle.

A Catechism for the Children of De-Light

Pagan individuals and cultures speak, remember, celebrate highly charged synchronistic events as giving direction to life. The depth and breadth of meaning within pagan realities is much more vast, much deeper than that available in the Cause/Effect scenarios of Westernized corporations, governments, religious and educational institutions. Decision-making about our future(s) utilizing connecting principles like synchronicity, would help humans live multidimensionally, less destructively, utilizing more of our incredible sensing potentials. Synchronistic directives, when followed, always appear to place an individual or culture within the proper grand ordering of the universe. 'Listening' for such directives is a primary subject taught by pagan Master teachers. One does not become a Master over Cause/Effect events. Instead one strives, through years of synchronistic experiences and the sharing of those experiences, to gain Wisdom. The sense of that Wisdom shared gives us the feeling of continual De-Light. Ultimately, each individual being experiences the complex openings of continual creation on all dimensions as we move from oneness into isolation and back toward oneness.

Awareness in decision-making based on Part VI

1. Causes have effects.
2. Belief in cause comforts.
3. Problems are generated by causal linking.
4. Problem solving limits.
5. Non-causal experience expands possibilities.

PART VII
PRINCIPLES OF GENDER

"From yon blue heavens above us bent, The gardener
Adam and his wife Smile at the claims of long descent."
— Alfred Lord Tennyson —

WHAT IS GENDER?

The notion of Gender is best expressed by the Greek 'stem gen' (genes), which implies birth, becoming, production, creation. Gender is the vehicle for De-Light, how De-Light manifests into our world. Polarities exist throughout all life (Part IV). Positive and negative energies are attached to our understandings of these polarities. When we name these charged energies, we utilize principles of correspondence and reflection (Part II). We call them masculine and feminine. Most importantly, we imbue these polarities with potential. From the union of female and male, life comes forth. Gender, i.e. the possibility of polarities coming together to produce, figures in a very primary way—biologically, physically, and metaphysically—in human awareness. All cultures, all institutions (including those of the current dominant culture), work in terms of Gender. Listening to human languages reveals how the presentation of information is related to gender. Tone, nuance, grammar, the subtleties of cultural understandings are all gender specific. Because we rely so heavily on Gender as our window to knowledge, many of the six principles previously discussed in this Catechism are veiled behind apparent male-female interaction. Even our notion of God(s) is usually Gender specific (Part 1).

WHAT ARE FEMALE AND MALE CHARACTERISTICS?

Humans celebrate the feminine as the Mother. She is receptive and giving-forth of life force energies. She nurtures and disciplines. She sustains. Through correspondence (Part II) our home on planet earth is the very embodiment of the power and complexity of the feminine.

Humans tend to revere the masculine as father. He is the spark, the creator of life which must manifest through the feminine. He is more powerful than nature or the feminine. Masculine force shapes, constructs, sculpts human destiny through word, image, institution, and incessant pushing-forth actions.

A Catechism for the Children of De-Light

Neither masculine nor feminine can bring forth life without partnership. Males, through the principles of correspondence, are of the air and fires. Females are of the water and earth. It takes creative mixing of these four elements for De-Light to manifest. It is around the union and disunion of male and female that all human cultural understandings therefore revolve.

HOW DO CULTURES AND INSTITUTIONS UTILIZE MALE-FEMALE CHARACTERISTICS?

It is around the principle of Gender that the Church, Mosque, Temple orthodoxy makes its most obvious separation with all pagan traditions. It is also around Gender that the dominant culture, controlled by international corporations, differs and vies for power with religious orthodoxy. Both the religious orthodoxies and the corporate culture share beliefs in a dualistic reality. For them Oneness, The ALL, contains a split along lines of Gender.

In this separation the Masculine-Feminine principles cease to be dynamic energies flowing in continual generation. They become rigid forms set in judgmental relationship to one another. Viewed from the distortion of that dualism all higher life, all manifestations of the Spirit or Soul, are seen as reflections of the masculine principle. All things of matter or body are feminine. Church, Mosque, Temple orthodoxy, in the business of domination of Soul-Spirit-Mind, have instituted whole formats of cultural practice passed on through language, ritual, liturgy, moral rules and law. Human behavior, according to these institutions, is supposed to reflect the male half of Gender.

God is a Father in all the orthodox traditions. He is the masculine force reflected by lightning or by the ram. He is the creator of matter. He is to be honored and obeyed as the giver of Law. The masculine principle is understood to be dominant. Everything is seen as moving to and from the masculine pole. He is Light. He is Right. He is perfection. Without Him, without Spirit, Matter would not be alive.

Because the Feminine force is equated with Matter in this duality, she is lesser. She is controlled by the masculine figurehead. Although she is necessary for creation and generation, she is only seen as necessary in a physical sense. Spirit generates itself and all else, including her. She is darkness. She is the temptress who pulls the masculine force down, away from its higher spiritual calling. She is incomplete. Although she may appeal to spirit in prayer, she will never find unity. She is seen and treated as a lesser factor in the orthodox spiritual life.

This duality has so permeated our consciousness that it makes it almost impossible to see beyond it. It is an extremely important factor locked into our languages, our images, our sense of how life functions. We must be continually alert to all the subtleties of this duality, for it lies at the root of many important human decisions about the future of how we live with our planet.

If all matter is understood as Feminine, and the feminine is seen as lesser, or even Evil, then what does that mean about Earth? If the feminine is seen as weaker, vulnerable, to be taken care of by humans, to be guided by humans, do these higher, masculine sensibilities really do any more than perpetuate human mismanagement? In the dualistic scheme of the orthodoxies and dominant culture, earth is the essence of matter as we know it. In their moralizing she is a dark temptation. She is of the realm of the serpentine, the lower forces, the devil. All physical bodies are fallen. All other life, plants, microbes and animals are lower than humans properly oriented toward Him. Earth is to be used, to satisfy needs, to provide human comfort. Earth is to be consumed in the glorification of Spirit, of Him.

Again it is almost impossible for us to get beyond some aspect of this dualism, even in our most holistic moments when we act as caretakers, recycles, promoters of using less and walking lightly.

IS THERE A WAY AROUND THE DUALISTIC GENDER TRAP?

To fully understand the fallacy of expression of masculine and feminine principles as dualism, we must return to the science of polarity. Matter understood as Energy is not separate from generative Spirit. Energy interactions are dimensionally complex.

Through correspondence the image of the core of energy life is the atom, composed of electrons, ions, or corpuscles, depending upon the terminology used. These entities are seen as revolving around each other and as being in continuous vibration. They are in a relationship of elasticity or tension. Each of their entities carries a positive and negative charge capability.

Scientists usually represent atom structure as the clustering of negative ions around a positive pole. Positive ions (or electrons or corpuscles) exert an influence upon the negative ions causing the negative ions to assume certain combinations. This is termed creation or generation of an atom. In other words, the masculine polarity is stronger than the feminine polarity. Clustering tends toward the masculine. Suns gather up planets, etc. And through correspondence we understand that the rest of the material world works in like manner.

It appears on the surface that the masculine pole is responsible for generating life, and thus is the primary cause (Part VI). As long as we talk in terms of Positive and Negative polarities and mean Masculine and Feminine, the negative is likely to be seen as weaker, dominated by the masculine or positive polarity. Many scientists have recognized that this picture of positive polarity dominance does not allow an accurate description of phenomenon. They have pointed out that using the terminology 'negative polarity' carries with it a prejudice of meaning; the term negative being associated with all that is wrong, bad, weak, in our dualistic modern culture. Instead they use the word Cathode to describe the activity of the Negative pole. Cathode has a Greek root meaning 'path of generation.'

Contemporary discussions of electrical energy understand the Cathode or Negatively charged pole as receiving electrons from an outside source of current during the process of electrolysis. The Cathode is the pole toward which cations migrate. Cations are electropositive, while Anions, or electro-negative ions, move to the anode or Positive pole.

In other words, *clustering* is not a phenomenon which is Masculine in nature. Nor is generation Masculine. The Cathode pole generates swarms of electrons, (ions or corpuscles.) And it generates Cathode rays, a stream of electrons which passes from the Cathode to the opposite wall of an evacuated electron tube, *when they are excited by a current or a series of spark discharges.* It is not the immediate positive-negative relationship, then, which is responsible for Cathode clustering. An outside source of stimulation is required. The Greeks named this outside force Zeus and gave him the power of Lightning, the sign of the Spark. Zeus is an exciter, a stimulator, but the power of generation is understood as a Feminine principle. Life comes from the Feminine Force. This principle is the basis for much of modern technology, including the cathode ray tubes in most television and computer screens.

Questions of the origins of the entire universe are raised in terms of Gender . Where does the 'spark' come from. What 'caused' the bang? Is the Lightning the primary source, or is there a greater emptiness, one or more dimensional levels of reality within which the spark happens? And is that reality feminine?

Creative or generative electrons (ions or corpuscles) carry feminine charge. They are composed of negative or feminine energy. In nature there is a process which we term ionization. In this process the feminine ion (Neg Ion) leaves a Masculine ion. She is the active, free, force. She moves away, always seeking a union with another masculine Ion. Scientific language is clear that it is the feminine ion which seeks a union of its own volition. The terminology of will power, or reasoned determination is ascribed to the motion of the Neg Ion. She is not drawn away. She is free in the sense that all choice is free, in a context of her greater nature. Her seeking nature is recognized as essential for vitality in Life. It is her continual surging, coming-forth, which we experience as De-Light.

Pagans recognize a similar will toward union, which resides within the Feminine principle. It is Her continual movements toward union, not union itself, which are essential to regeneration. The element of continual change, which makes each moment new and different, is a result of this Feminine seeking.

When a union is accomplished, another process begins. The Feminine Ion, (electron or corpuscle) vibrates, rapidly, when it nears a Masculine energy field. Feminine ions circle at great speeds around Masculine Ions. The result is the birth of new atomic particles.

Everything which is a manifestation of the ALL corresponds to this principle of generative creation. Fertility arises from the Feminine seeking and moving toward a union. What appear as Female Fertility cults honoring a Goddess are in fact recognitions of this generative principle.

Detached ions (electrons or corpuscles) are the most active forces in nature. These feminine charges are responsible for the feeling we get of freshness in our atmosphere. High concentrations of Neg Ions promote health, vitality and well being. On the other hand, Pos Ions with a masculine charge are not good when they are in great concentration. Pos Ion poisoning is a severe problem in specific localities around the planet. The effects of Pos Ion poisoning have been studied, and include the breakdown of antibody systems in many organisms with accompanying weakness which can lead to susceptibility to all kinds of disease. Neg Ions (the feminine forces) counteract the Positive Ionization tendencies in our mineral laden atmosphere. Neg Ions are light, airy. They are the energies one feels beside a waterfall or at the ocean or in the woods. They are healing energies, moving a sluggish body from lethargy. In soils, a heightened cation exchange (movement of Neg Ions) is a key to fertility.

The continual unions formed by the movement of the Feminine Ions (electrons or corpuscles) with their Masculine counterparts are the basis for all phenomenon, including light, heat, magnetism, chemical and biological organisms, and all human thoughts.

The human body should be of a condition that allows the free movement of Feminine electrons. In this condition the nerve endings vibrate rapidly, and attunement with other vibrating bodies is possible. For whatever reason, if rigidity becomes the general state of a Human or any other life form, then sickness occurs. Since the energies of our thoughts are intricately woven into all physical manifestations, the principle of the detached Feminine seeker should always be the condition of our consciousness. When we hold to Forms, Structures or Conceptions which are the results of unions (of positive and negative energies) and don't allow for continually new and different unions to occur, we become frozen, locked in stasis. The frozen state is at best Life-On-Hold. At worst it approaches anti-life.

IS MENTAL AWARENESS GENDER SPECIFIC?

Western conceptions allow us to speak as if mind and its mental aspects are separate from the body, the physical, the spirit, from all other life processes. Once we allow that dualistic split in our speech, other terminologies follow. They are generally given meaning by assigning them Gender names. Consciousness and unconsciousness are usually given masculine and feminine correspondences. Consciousness is thought of as 'of the light' and masculine. Unconsciousness is seen as 'of the dark,' the mysterious, the unknown, the hidden—the feminine. Because of the hierarchical nature of the Mind-Matter split in the West, consciousness (masculine) is favored over unconsciousness (feminine). In nonwestern and particularly pagan cultures, however, the dimensional worlds of the unknown, of dreams, unseen phenomena, etc. are given at least as much radiance as those which are seen, known, understood.

Furthermore, in the Western or dominant culture of our era, it is usually understood that consciousness should control unconsciousness. The unconscious is unruly. She is in fact a free force always seeking union with the conscious, but dangerously corruptive of it. Unconscious information is allowed to 'surface,' but it is rapidly relegated to the realms of the Arts, or the babbling of mental patients, or 'occult' metaphysics. The Arts and metaphysical pronouncements are seen as of feminine energy. Science is trusted as 'factual,' thus more appropriately masculine. In decision-making, Gender plays a huge role as we need to rely on information derived from masculine, rational, conscious sources. Artistic or metaphysical information derived from non-rational sources may be given praise as beauty or being lively, but is not relevant to how we generally run our world. Just as feminine source opinions have been traditionally second class or nonexistent in dominant culture decision-making, so information from the hidden, unknown sides of our natures (within the dualism) is deemed suspect, lower, even evil in content.

IS THERE A WAY TO EMBRACE THE PARADOX OF GENDER?

Many pagan practices appear to combine Masculine and Feminine in a unified Being represented by an Androgynous form. Through principles of correspondence and reflection this kind of unity is reflected for human awareness by everything from flowers to worms. Both the female and the male are active generative forces within one clustering. We do not speak of an Androgynous Being without knowledge that somehow the paradoxical nature of male and female can be balanced, one usually a little more active, a little more dominant than the other. Humans who strive for androgyny are usually not hermaphroditic in a sexual sense. Rather, the recognition that gender is only one way of defining who we are, points us towards appreciation of energy complexities, allows us to see and be in a condition of continual amazement at the vast nature of each being.

A Catechism for the Children of De-Light

In pagan cultures the principle of Gender often appears to take precedence over other principles. Many icons depict the interplay of the Masculine and Feminine. In the dualistic West we tend not to see this male-female activity honored. In fact, its prominence in cultural practices or art is likely to bring cries of pornography.

In this Catechism we have probed seven basic commonly used principles which permeate all pagan and orthodox understandings. If we look at these principles from the point of view of the dominant, mainly Western culture, we will see that Feminine Gender is clustered with Vibration and Rhythm and these are seen as lesser influences in the ordering of the world.

Masculine	Feminine
Oneness	Vibration
Correspondence	Rhythm
Polarity	Gender
Cause	

This catechism is dedicated to the children of De-Light. It therefore speaks from the Feminine, the activating, continual-creation, energy-giving side of our understandings. Prominence is given to the principles of Gender, Vibration and Rhythm. Most other catechisms weigh the masculine side of this duality in their presentation of the ordering principles of reality. That is a crucial difference.

If you weigh the role of the Masculine Principles, then the seventh (or first) principle, which is Oneness or God, appears as Masculine. However, Gender itself carries a Feminine vibration. For in the light of full consideration Oneness includes Gender. Feminine characteristics are necessary for continual Creation. The masculine cannot exist alone, ever, nor can it act in a exclusively primary sense where Life is concerned.

The Church, Mosque and Temple complexes have recognized this. They are much more likely to consider fully the implications of Correspondences, Polarities, and Causes than they are Gender. For a consideration of Gender moves them into a trap as they consider the All, or One, or Spirit God. If the God or Oneness principle is seen in terms of energy, it is obvious that it is All masculine and All feminine. One Gender is not derivative of the other. Eve is not Adam's rib. It might be closer to the actual case to say that Adam is dead without Eve's presence. Both are necessary for there to be life.

God is not exclusively HIM for the Pagan. Nor is God exclusively HER. Depending upon the vibrational context in which God is invoked, terms like Mother-Father might be spoken. When God has been understood in her feminine aspect, it is always made clear that she acts in consort with her masculine counterpart. For pagans it is also clear that the Godhead as masculine can function only in consort with the feminine Goddess.

There have been times when individuals within the Church, Mosque and Temple complexes who have considered God vibrationally, rhythmically, as well as in terms that embrace the androgynous whole. But the institutions themselves usually crush individuals who worship this balance. Any gender balance threatens patriarchal institutional superiority. Even when male centered control is deemed inappropriate (as in the last decades of the 20th century) male dominance is maintained by clever machinations of language, by mesmerizing the masses until they are no longer alert to how they are being controlled. Physical force, the collusion of religious and military, are used to maintain superiority when other practices fall. It is Gender imbalance that reigns around decision-making tables as we humans continue to use-up the planetary Mother's 'resources.'

WHY IS HUMAN SEXUALITY SO CENTRAL TO PAGAN CULTURES?

Gender unification is celebrated through total human merging. Principles of seeming universal duality are really functions of masculine-feminine interplay. Even the smallest atom and the greatest star systems are understood as having life because of the sexual nature of the universe.

A Catechism for the Children of De-Light

Human sexuality has been a primary focus of sacred understanding for pagan cultures as long as there have been people. Icon, decoration, sculpted forms shaped of stone, the long lasting essence of Earth Mother, all tell us the story of how people have seen themselves alive and creating in a sexual reality. The sensuous nature of humans is never suppressed in pagan cultures. The body is not separate from the spirit, but is a mirror through which can be discovered all that is. Enlightenment or fulfillment can be manifested through a careful development of sexuality.

Human sexuality is cosmic union. It is not merely physical copulation. It is a total merging of energies. It is vibratory, rhythmic, the feminine principles activated to balance the male principles. Pagan cosmology is sexual. It is achieved in human sexual union when that union is done as ceremony, celebration of all that is. The two-made-one is not relegated to institutions of any kind. It is dynamic interaction, daily, dimensionally, between genders. Sexuality is even within all that we speak. All our forms of language, written, painted, photographed, danced, toned through instruments, are sexual, moment to moment expressions of the two coming together as one.

For this reason sexual development in a human individual is carefully guided. The dynamic interplay of female and male forces is the cornerstone in pagan cultures of much story-teaching and ritual-teaching. When a whole cosmology is understood to be expressed though each individual and communal human action, when all is sacred, moment to moment alertness is required.

Contrast this to the way gender is typically handled by the dominant culture and the Church, Mosque and Temple complexes. Sexuality has been suppressed by these institutions. Or in the case of the popular images of the modern dominant culture, sexuality is twisted, made bizarre by emphasizing the human body as a sellable thing. Prostitution exists subtlety as a cornerstone of all levels of modern market economies. Religious institutions with secular legal counterparts turn sexuality into laws, sanctioned practices, including legal marriage to one sexual partner. In their most severe interpretation religious institutions have sanctioned only procreation. All other forms of sexual practice have been banned, been causes for condemnation both in this life and in afterlife scenarios.

In the orthodoxy and in the dominant culture the language of male dominance continues to reign. Legal copulation is often defined as the male sexual muscle penetrating the female sexual opening, releasing sperm necessary for fertilization the continuation of generations. The proper position for women in this scenario is submissive. The male aggressor does 'it' to the female. In such 'love-making' the dualistic split between male and female is maintained, but is allowed a monetary bridging. The continuation of male dominance, through the production of sons, is the primary purpose of copulative action. When it is accomplished, the union is broken. New life begun, there is no reason for copulation until another life giving session is ordained. Through correspondence, it is understood that God thrust Himself into the universe in a similar creative fashion. The Earth or Garden was given life by Him. This act was performed once as a causal line to the necessary process of procreation.

For pagans sexual fulfillment is not a reinstatement of mastery over the feminine forces. It is a celebration of continual creative principles, of De-Light. It is understood that heightened vibration within the All is the key to health and well-being throughout all creation. One sexual act is not isolated from the All. It is necessary for the continual vibrational well-being of All.

Rhythms bringing about oneness within the feminine, often experienced as a series of rolling orgasms, are physical indications that celebration through touch and energy sharing has reached full communion with the ALL. Earthquakes might be understood as similar celebrations of feminine continual creative force. In the female human body it is known that the clitoris, the miniature reflection of the male penis, is the energy center most sensitive to rhythms which bring about amplified vibrational characteristics.

A Catechism for the Children of De-Light

The vaginal lips, the entry to the cave, reflected in Earth caves, are likewise very sensitive vibration surfaces. Sexual interplay between partners is physical, alert to physical stimulation. But focus on subtle clusters of energy sharing is the real essence of sexual celebration. The therapeutic healing effect of this interplay affects everything, including growth patterns of all other beings, in addition to their well being. Subtle sexual energy sharing therefore helps in the creation of food, shelter and clothing.

The orthodox Church, Mosque and Temple have at various times defined sexual actions of a vibrational nature as 'unnatural.' At crucial periods in their quest for power they have gone so far as to have the clitoris cut from women so that these vibrational sexual celebrations could not be realized. Human sexuality that is anything other than copulation for procreation has been punished as wicked and indulgent. People engaging in such practices are deemed sinful, fornicators, subject to torture and death.

This sexual activity, which has been deemed unnatural, has gone "behind closed doors" away from the eyes of the orthodoxy and legal authorities. Suppressive attitudes dampen the element of celebration of what is really natural sexual expression, making the masses of people weak through guilt and fear, while promoting an authoritarian control. Historically, sensitive sexual practices have been linked to stories of the city of Sodom, which was destroyed because of such wicked practices. These practices became codified into law, the crime of sodomy carrying a stiff sentence in many countries.

The sacredness of Gender has outraged the Church, Mosque and Temple complexes more than any other aspect of pagan belief and practice. Artistic representations of sexual consorts, even the ritual and ceremonial centers used by Goddess worshipers, have been smashed and burned, their true meaning twisted. This has suppressed or destroyed traditional knowledge of the heightening of feminine vibration, all of which should have been passed from generation to generation as a cultural gift. But to allow ONE-NESS of Gender threatens the patriarchal orthodoxies more than any other activity, since it exposes their organized authority as having no basis in the natural interplay of the universal ALL. Only with the separation of the body from the spiritual can they stay in power.

DOESN'T MOTHER MARY BALANCE MASCULINE CHURCH POWER?

In the Christian tradition Mary is deified. Throughout Europe and the Americas statues and cathedrals are dedicated to her presence. She was the Mother necessary for the church to exist.

The Christ figure himself, perhaps ironically, takes up some of the feminine vibrational roles. His message is of Love. He counsels us to turn the other cheek when we are in a masculine or confrontational situation. Through faith, magic acts upon the stuff of the world—loaves and fishes—and multitudes are fed. But these feminine aspects have a distinctly masculine tone. Christ was not a Woman. To gain pagans into its fold, the Church instituted Mary as a feminine figure worthy of worship. However, this worth did not extend equality. Her fame is because she submitted to God the Father's will and brought forth his only son. There was never a chance for God the Father and Christ the Mother or consort. Such a conception might have balanced the energy equation, but it would have undermined the Church's patriarchal quest for power.

IS GENDER A KEY TO HOW WE LIVE IN TECHNOLOGICAL TIME?

Both male and female vibrations must be celebrated for life to become whole and healthy. Traditionally, however, we understand the penetrating rays of Sun, the timing effects of Sun as masculine, and the receptive, birthing effects of Earth as feminine. What is our relationship to Her? Is she daughter, the potential for future life? Is she Mother, bearing us and nurturing us? Or is she our Grandmother, showing us through signs, Her wisdom regarding the life process?

A Catechism for the Children of De-Light

If we regard Earth as submissive to human will, for a while she will respond. She will give-up her body, her resources. Her children will appear wealthy, lavishly adorned, with social norms based upon the manipulation of her resources into mega-tons of technological trinkets. But Earth is the feminine principle. As such she is always on the move. She is Change. She will be different when we have emptied her of non-renewable resource. She will be different when her veins are loaded with poisons to the point of sterility. She will no longer be daughter ripe with potential life, or mother giving life when those limits are reached. In that used-up condition she might be more akin to the traditional notion of the Hag, a malicious feminine force, who must resort to sorcery to right conditions that are out of balance.

The choice is in our hands and hearts. We have taken the role of managers of the Earth at this time. If we were to chose to once again relate to her vibrationally (vibration ally), as more than our equal in on-going-life-generating, then our daily lives would change, radically. Her rapid motions can move us toward a softening, toward a slowing of pace, toward appreciation of the incredible complexity that is within each moment. Our decisions would be unions of female and male energy, part of the natural celebrations of De-Light flowing the totality of the ALL.

Awareness in decision-making based on Part VII
1. What is female or male reflects contexts.
2. Clustering and discharge are elemental.
3. Neg ions freshen, rebalance.
4. Gender associations render us judgmental.

PART VIII
PRINCIPLES OF DIRECTION

A Catechism for the Children of De-Light

WHERE ARE WE?

We come into human form while swimming in the waters of Mother. We come from within Mother. Suddenly, there is a world of Light. We cry. We are born to life unattached, one very complex energized being among all the other beings of the universe and earth. We wonder where we are.

We stay attached for an extended period of time, Mother nourishing, nurturing. But gradually we venture out. Parents and community, guardians who know, give us structures and guidance within which we explore and discover this earth reality. At the same time we experience simple sensations that are all important to knowing who and where we are. We breathe. We move. We become aware that other beings breathe and move. We experience Air. We crawl and have our first experiences with Earth. We are bathed and taken into rain or snow and have our awakenings to Water. Fire, the energy within us that drives our emotions, is experienced even within the watery womb. Humans structure each other with the Wisdom of these four basic elements. What we are is them: Earth our bodies, Water our blood, Air our spirit, and Fire our continual De-Light.

How we know where we are is an extension of these four sensations. Sometimes we learn from the four winds. The South wind is warm, moist, sometimes delicate, cuddly, like mother holding us and comforting us. From the West comes the wind of change. It is often fierce, dark, sometimes scary, but transformative. From the North cold winds come, freezing over all the warmth, forcing us to live in starkness, alert to basic patterns for survival. From the East come circling winds or sometimes winds of extreme clarity. The winds of this direction are a combination of the other three winds and feel like the dawn looks, new and alive with potential.

We know where we are because our earth spins in relation to our sun, we experience light and dark, dawn and sunset. We experience sunlight moving north and south relative to our planetary position, creating the seasons. We know that East is the place where the sun appears to rise in the morning and West is the place where it appears to disappear in the evening.

We learn that many of our feathered kin fly in flocks along pathways invisible to us but genetically familiar to them. They make these migrations with the seasons, moving North for summer and South for winter. If we did no more than follow the migrating birds, we would know the directions of magnetic north and south, the extreme polarities of Earth.

We know where we are by the elements living around us. But we know that on Earth we have come from within, from within our Mother's warm, moist gestation and growth place. At a cellular level, we know that we came from father sperm and mother egg united in De-Light, making a new being. All the genetic coding within that union informs us of other lives spent in creative discovery and survival by other beings who shared their blood, body, spirit, energy sources to continue the upwelling of the creative force. These family ties are alive within us, orient us. We know where we are when we are around others who carry this same genetic information or similar information. We know where we are because we are of family. And that family comes from within.

WHY IS A SENSE OF PLACE IMPORTANT?

We come from our centers outward. Out there is a strange world. We interact with it helplessly at first. As we grow into that world we learn ever wider parameters. First we learn Mother. Then Father. Then dwelling, or these days hospital or institution where birthing takes place. That our first sense of place might be days of institutional surfaces, noises, the buzzing of man-made electrical background energy means we enter a world quite different from a child born quietly at home, or a child born of a mother who goes away from harvest in a field into a wood, by herself or with a sister to give birth with the winds and weather of that day, with the sounds of birds and perhaps water flowing in a stream. We grow from our centers outward, like rings in a tree. But when we retreat to that center for nourishment, for orientation, what we find may be very different from what we would like to find simply because our Mother location probably exists within the modern, industrial world, a reflection of the dominant culture rather than a more natural condition. Our center, our basic location, is more likely to be fear-filled if our birth was in an institutional setting, or more likely to be calm if our mother lived and birthed with nature.

Each of us humans needs to feel our center alive, bubbling out from the source, becoming the stream that is our rushing lives. We need to feel that center daily. It is the source of our particular balance, well being, our way, as we move through all the other energies that surround and penetrate us. Like turtles, we carry our centers with us. Yet, to return to our centers means a return to place, usually *a place*. Home on this earth is a place where we can re-center. Home is a place where De-Light can happen without interference, danger, or overpowering forces corrupting free flowing energy. Home can be shared in spirit, around Fire, but real home, home where we feel our place in this life on this earth, is not shared. Home is the total connection of the center within our core to a place outside ourselves. Home may be a spot on a floor where you sit each day to meditate. It may be a path through a wood. Wherever it is, home allows us to be inward-looking, safe from the continual alertness that is demanded by the modern world. Without home, we feel lonely, like we don't belong to this planetary life. The distractions provided by the dominant culture, such as television, computer technologies, high-speed air and ground transportation systems, block or sway our sense of home off-center. So pervasive has the dominant culture become, that we often have no sense of center, of home, of being able to feel all the creative energy of De-Light. In that overpowered position individuals suffer. Their cells react, become unhealthy. Without a sense of place, of center, continual sickness keeps humans at the mercy of those in the dominant culture who would sell them cures. Of course the only cure is ultimately to find your center and maintain it, daily.

CAN SACRED PLACES HELP
WITH HUMAN CENTERING?

There are many kinds of sacred places, places designated by various cultures as safe zones, places where an individual can freely commune with spirit. Some of these places exist in nature and are frequented by all kinds of animals, including humans. In those places you feel powerful energies resulting from how Earth centers herself. Pathways or lines of wave energies cross at points. Some of these forces are within earth herself. Some are in her atmosphere. Where crossings happen sensitive humans have established shrines, temples, mosques and cathedrals. Tribal societies reserve these places for sacred ceremony. Prayers, visions, councils with all the beings of all dimensional realities take place in these places.

Going to a sacred place to find your center usually has the effect of giving you a particular language to describe your centering experience. If you go to a known vision quest place, what you sense, feel, see is likely to be understood in terms of the native culture of that area. If you go to a Cathedral located on the same place only several hundred years later, then even though you are doing a centering activity, the language of interpretation is likely to be that of the church. Each sacred place language interpretation is not our actual centering, although we often speak as if it is. The pure energy of that sacred place is experienced differently by each person. Speaking the truths of our personal centering is difficult because languages always entrap us in culture(s) blocking the full effects of De-Light as it wells up through us in a particular place.

In sacred places ritual always includes elements of the four principle ingredients of Earth experience: Earth, Water, Air and Fire. How these elements are experienced in the cultural history of a sacred place sets in motion all the complexity of that culture's orthodoxy, beliefs, creeds, dogmas, truths and doctrines. Prayerful worship, the proper human attitude in a sacred place, is defined respect for the interpretation of the four elements within that sacred place, structure, area. The altar created by the sacred pipe is an interpretation every bit as valid and as human as the altar created with the cross or with the ark of the convent.

Finding a place alone to experience centering and the force of De-Light coming through our personal centering becomes more difficult as humans populate ever greater areas of earth. For an urbanite it is perhaps best to establish your centering place where you live. It may only be a spot on a floor. But if you practice centering, opening yourself to De-Light daily on that spot, the energy of that centering will remain with that place. The place will become charged. It will become somewhat easier for you to work with your core on that one place. As we become stronger, able to gather and decimate more intense magnitudes of De-Light energy, we can charge other places we frequent, such as a desk in an office. In these charged places we continue to gather and flow. We attract. People gather round us, not knowing why. We process loads of displaced energy. We become healers amongst those who feel dysfunctional, lost, unable to find their centers in a world that distracts.

WHY IS IT NECESSARY TO INVOKE THE FOUR DIRECTIONS OR ELEMENTS?

Most human cultures invoke, in ceremony, ritual, liturgy and prayer, the four directions as they are experienced on Earth. Sometimes this is voiced. Among the natives of the Americas, Africa, Mongolia, and Lapland, for instance, the powers associated with North, South, East and West are called upon to aid with well-being, healing, teaching and a feeling of unity with all our relations on this planet. In the songs of Tibetan monks the elements associated with the four directions and the colors symbolically representing those directions are everywhere, even on clothing. Throughout Europe the Old Way surfaces through the structures and signs of the dominant Christian culture. The sign of the cross is itself a reflection of the power of the knowledge of four directions. Priests during mass express this power each time they genuflect, cross themselves, the elements of the mass, the gathered people all doing the same. Within the trinity of Father, Son, Holy Spirit there is a fourth, rarely mentioned, life force or De-Light. People who grow up bi-culturally, knowing the four directions as basic creature understanding and action, but celebrating the mass with Christians, are aware that the sign of the cross is the sign of the four.

It is necessary to consciously enact the sign of the four, or cry out to the four, because that defines our place in the flux of continual creative growth in that moment. The four directions orient us. We are never lost when we know that we are the center, the moving center, of all the magnetic forces we experience. Power is a function of relationship. But there can be no true relationship with another being if we don't know where we are.

It may seem simple to note our sense of place by the apparent sunrise and sunset, the migrations of birds and other beings along magnetic pathways and the sun's path, North then South. But this knowledge is basic, fundamental to our being with all other beings, for they also share this knowledge. Moss, trees, grasses, flowers inhabit places where life is best for them. Their presence in those places 'tells' us about the power of that place, its orientation. Pagan peoples who are continually alert to the presence of orientation among all the other beings, with whom we share earth, move in a world of silent but powerful communication. Even the rocks, by how they weather, and with their unique placements, 'talk' to us of where they are, therefore where we are.

WHY DO DIFFERENT PEOPLES ASSOCIATE VARIANT COLORS WITH THE FOUR DIRECTIONS?

Most cultures associate sunrise in the East with bright colors. Sometimes this color is symbolically yellow. Sometimes red or red orange. The blaze of the dawning sun brings light into darkness, lifting our energies to embrace the cellular and magnetic interactions that will happen as a result of sun-light presence that day. In all the paintings, weavings, beadwork, and other visual expressions of the four directions, bright sunrise colors usually invoke the East.

Most cultures associate sunset in the West with coming darkness. Darker colors represent the power of light going away into the great mystery of night. Starlight and reflected moonlight provide a glow during the night. We are given, even in darkness, direction—very beautiful direction. All the cultural stories and forms projected among the stars (constellations) are expressions of orientation within darkness. The phases of the moons help us sense direction as their energies change over twelve cycles before they repeat season. Many symbolic representations of the West convey a darkness within which exists brilliance; bright, sometimes fiery colors appear. These are representations of reflected light, different from but no less creative and giving than the dazzling sunlight. Many cultures associate the dark West with storms, fear or death, for all these earth actions also have a place. Other associations include the practice of "looking-within" of "living with heart," of opening secrets and magic, as our individual centering is an 'inner' process at the same time that it is an 'outer' process.

The colors associated with the South vary widely, even within cultures. Usually they are blues, greens, yellows or even white associated with earth as garden. Primal earth life is filled with teachings uncorrupted by human intervention. The waters, trees and grasses nourish other smaller creatures who play and reproduce among them. Among native peoples there are legendary trickster characters who teach by leading all theses beings from innocence toward knowledge of how to exist with all other beings. Coyote, Rabbit, Raven, Fox, attempt to lead us to understand our world by manipulating the beings and the colors of the south. Scientists and technicians serve that function in modern industrial cultures. Their knowledge is ever changing, moved by collective fad, foisted upon a non-alert populace of beings who unfortunately mismanage with that seeming knowledge.

A Catechism for the Children of De-Light

Wisdom, which is quite different from knowledge, and is associated with having lived long and seen much, is generally placed in the North. Usually the colors associated with the North are the white of snows and cold, of white hairs on the old ones among the animals (including humans) who have lived long and have perspective. Some cultures use purples or reds to convey the northern direction. Symbolically, it is important to recognize the colors of the beings who live within the snowy condition. Certain conifers, or sometimes small plants with bright colored berries, even animals, indigenous to the North, change their coloring to become white in Winter so that they are less visible in the snowy, iced-over condition. The northern lights, those mysterious wisps of sky color in the permanent dark of polar night show us that subtle energies can be visible. These brilliant, ever changing, sky-colors reflect how earth herself is magnetically charged, how all creatures and beings are complex, interactive, magnetic energies. Within the fields of frozen white all the pastel colors of that energy-dance exist.

Human color-consciousness gives us direction, daily, subtly. We do not paint, bead, weave, without invoking the four directions. When we do these processes with intention, then the power of the directions moves through us like the four winds. Each of us is an artist, daily. How we dress, wear jewelry, look at a flower, tells us how complex or unformed is our sense of direction of where we are. If we remember the colors as they are given by life around us, then everywhere, every moment, the colors teach, tell us what life is about. The language of life resides in the colors of the four directions.

DO THE FOUR DIRECTIONS ORIENT US ONLY ON EARTH?

In Part II correspondence points us to understand that our orientation on Earth would also be true above, in the sky, in other ethereal worlds; and below, in the earth, in the depths of oceans, in worlds that are of earth but are also of myth and legend. Pagan cultures created stories of travel and adventure in these other worlds, and in so doing, they anthropomorphized these realms of totally other dimensional energy. For the Greeks, Romans, Polynesians, Persians and many others, the heavens were, and are, places of wonder, peopled with well known gods, goddesses, monsters, storms, beauty, all of the relations of earth. Telling these stories, season after season, around fires and eventually in theaters, and books and now with movies and television, teaches us the principles that are written down in this catechism.

In Pagan cultures there are many worlds, but there are three that are invoked in ceremony and prayer. There is this world, i.e. the material world, which is not really solid, but is filled with individual energies all in relationship. There is the world above, a place of spirits, angels and ethereal beings able to move and interact with earthlings without regard to physical boundary. Yet, these beings are recognizable as forms known on earth. Some appear winged, but so do birds. Some appear to be genetically crossed, part human, part horse, part bird, but the parts are familiar earth forms, even if the being is a hybrid, a product of mythic genetic engineering.

The places inhabited by beings of the world above or outside this world are not simply figments of human imagination. This is a very important cornerstone in understanding pagan consciousness. The realms of the sky are filled with entities. These spirit forms interact with earth beings. They are vibrating at a more intense level. Therefore they are able to direct those of us who are of slower vibration. They are able to guide us, teach us, show us where we are going. For yes, they do operate within the four directions.

These beings and their guides and teachers are invoked by pagan peoples in prayers, ceremonies and rituals. That invocation constitutes a fifth direction. In those invocations relationship is re-established. We ask that those with greater vibrational awareness be presence as guides and teachers during our unfoldment, our movement from our centers outward. At the same time we ask, we give. We give them presence in our personal earth lives.

A Catechism for the Children of De-Light

A third world, a sixth direction is invoked by pagans who are aware that Earth herself holds other whole dimensions of life. She gives us life, but she offers more if we are willing to explore her depths. Within her reside all kinds of entities, vibrational forms, which we tend to anthropomorphize in order to understand. Some of these beings exist mythically in realms of fire, steam, underground waterways. They inhabit deep caves and caverns and are of the volcanoes and underwater breathing holes of earth. Their emissaries are often water creatures, monsters, hidden energies that manifest suddenly. They can be frightening because they come from the realms of the dark that are not illumined with starlight.

In our era we have named many invisible creatures that are biologically, chemically, physically necessary for life on earth. Primordial bacteria, fungus, algae, and many more members of what I refer to as the 'micro-herd' interact with minerals and plant acids and create the fertile garden we envision as Eden or earth at her lushest. In pagan circles we invoke the energies of all these beings. And we give to them. For we as humans are transmitters. We stand in the middle between the worlds above and the worlds below. Like trees, our spirits are rooted and reaching. We often pray standing, palms up, arms raised to the heavens, feet spread, planted into the earth, letting all the energies of all our relations flow through us. Ironically many priests pray in similar position while their parishioners kneel.

Most pagan circles invoke a seventh direction. It is the center, who we are, where we are, the fire and the heightened vibrational energy that is the result of merging our energy-field-selves with all the energies of all the beings in the dimensions in six directions. We grow from the center outward as we are birthed from our Mother. So we grow from the center outward as we re-energize, celebrating the De-Light that is life.

We are capable of projecting our energy fields away from earth, out into the planets of the solar system, beyond into other star systems. Very powerful shamanistic practitioners have experienced what is only beginning to be glimpsed by high-tech satellites, probes, and eventual human landings. Individuals whose energies have been gathered in alignments different from those experienced by most people have visited with 'entities' who exist dimensionally in fields created by other terrestrial bodies, planets in our sun's system and planets in the fields of other suns.

These visitations appear to even the advanced human energy field as reflections of our earth orientation, within four directions, within bands of color, shape, language that we understand. Initial encounters may be entirely outside the principles portrayed in this Catechism, but to interpret those encounters we rely on what we know. Many pagan peoples tell stories that say we humanoids actually came from the stars, from someplace other than this earth, historically, at some beginning, and at conception as the energy field accompanies the meeting of sperm with egg.

WHAT OF THE EIGHT AND THE TWELVE?

Buddhists teach the eight fold path. The Native American sundance lodge and brother lodge reflect the power of the twelve. All of these traditions in all cultures including African, Australian, Polynesian, Celtic, Nordic are extremely complex understandings woven in language, ritual, ceremony around the basic four directions. There are many, many interpretations. For instance, most cultures establish that four races were placed in four directions on our plane. Many peoples tell stories that reflect an understanding of the twelve tribes of humans. How each person, family, clan, village, tribe, people interpret and pass along stories of that complexity, makes humans seem different. Many wars, much bloodshed has taken place because of intolerance of how we interpret our place on this earth. If we understand the four, we can most easily find agreement. If we merge all our energies utilizing the four, pray together, work with all life together, celebrating continual De-Light rather than continual mishap, daily degradation, apparent death, then we can be what we are truly here to be, transmitters within which many dimensionally specific energized worlds meet, are charged, and re-emerge among all other creatures.

A Catechism for the Children of De-Light

DO THE FOUR DIRECTIONS ORIENT US IN DEATH?

Shedding the material body is our most primary life lesson. How we understand that passing, how we have oriented our energy fields toward merging with other dimensions of reality has much to do with who we are as we pass on, where we go, how we might reemerge into another material form, or how we might remain vibrating at a speedier-than-material-form-energy-pattern.

Most cultures interpret worlds after death in anthropomorphic and four directional metaphor. Many cultures even establish place in terms of higher, purer states or lower, more scary states. We try to understand what is to come after life with the language tools at hand. If those tools are trapped in dualism, then death is likely to be seen as an ending. Afterlife is likely to be seen in terms of reward and punishment for earthly deeds. If, however, dualism is overcome, if we understand and are open to De-Light emerging creatively through us, through our peculiar identities, then life flows continually. It may be that like an individual droplet of water we go down stream again and again and again. Or it may be that we become some other form of energy, maybe even beyond our current abilities to envision, understand, let-go-into.

We come into this life to learn. The learning is very complex and very simple. It is always limited by our abilities to sense totality, then to form languages and visual patterns to express that sensing. For humans, knowledge of death is always couched in four-directional terms, simply because that is how we are oriented, culturally.

Awareness in decision-making based on Part VIII

1. Place tends to shape context.
2. Direction(s) give quality.
3. Directions orient.
4. Cultures are based on orientation.

PART IX
PRINCIPLES OF
DIMENSION

"The human mind is unable to conceive of the four dimensions. How can it conceive of a God, before whom a thousand years and a thousand dimensions are as one?
— Albert Einstein - *On Science* —

A Catechism for the Children of De-Light

WHAT IS DIMENSION?

Continually creative De-Light energy is unseen, yet, we sense its presence. The world that is visual to humans is for the most part seen. It is filled with objects that are a function of Space. How we perceive occupation of Space is dimension.

One dimensional space is most easily understood as a dot occupying a place. If that dot does not generate motion of any kind, one dimensional existence is a possibility. However, as soon as that dot moves, it leaves a trace. That trace is understood as a line.

A line has a beginning and an end. A line is a connective. It connects polarities. Two dimensional space (2D) is an awareness of beginning and end and of the connective between. A two dimensional world is a world of surfaces. We could fall off such a world. Two dimensional reality appears cartoon-like.

If that two dimensional world moves, up or down, in or out, it leaves a trace. That trace shows us depth, volume. Moving lines generate three dimensional (3D) solids. Most of the time humans perceive the physical world as having depth or three dimensions. Our languages reflect this perception.

What happens when three dimensional occupation of space moves? It leaves a trace. That trace points toward a fourth dimension. What is the essence of that fourth dimension? Conceive of a dimension in which motion itself moves. Space and motion are one. Motion has direction. In our three-dimensional-world languages we conceive of motion-in-motion in space. When Space and Time are a continuum, three dimensional reality ceases to be merely visual. The world we know becomes the energy of which it is made. It is no longer solid. All that appears solid is in continual motion, is itself energy in motion. When we sense these moving energies, we experience De-Light.

Fourth dimension (4D) connectives can be seen, as though they were within 3D reality. This can happen when human brain wave energies are altered, moved out of habitual patterning. Dreams, deep meditations, certain dances, and hallucinogenic plants all help us get beyond "normal" or usual perception abilities. Much of the teaching, ritual and ceremony among pagan cultures is oriented toward training human consciousness to be aware, to be receptive, to experience 4D connective realities. For, once all of creation is experienced as energy connections and interactions, three 3D and 2D conceptions, including languages, institutions, relationships or political patterns, appear as limitation, possibly unnecessary, distractions, clouding or blocking 4D possibilities.

WHAT ARE LIMITS?

The capacity for human perception to function within the fourth dimension requires that the human instrument be itself totally within free-flowing-creative energies. To move and be as energy, we are receptive, open, engaging, totally interactive. We usually talk of this mode of sensing as innocence, trust. We mean by those words that a human in such an open mode has not suffered the intrusions, scaring, torture of negative interactions. For it is generally assumed that daily life is harsh and will result in individual beings closing their abilities to be totally interactive. We learn over time to protect ourselves. In the dominant culture setting up walls, or energy protections, is most often a function of instilled fear(s). Fears generate feelings of ownership, possession, reliance on authorities.

Energy limits are like spatial structuring. Human conception constructs those limits. Some are material forms. Buildings are limited energy forms, their shape and function defining realities inside and outside them. A house is very different from a cathedral; a teepee is not a coliseum. Each building shapes the activities they hold, defining space. Urban areas limit energy in different ways than rural areas. Air traffic can be a limiting factor in even the most remote areas, mechanical intrusion within primal quiet. Noise of all kinds forms a background roaring so pervasive that most modern humans are not aware of that noise as intrusion.

Some limitation is psychological or conceptual. The human brain grows patterns, habits, ways of understanding. Fresh creative energies are stopped or turned from what they are to what is more familiar by conscious and unconscious brain activity. The process of recognition—attempting to contain or fit our experience into our existing definitions and understanding—limits free flowing De-Light energy. We approach language limits whenever we try to talk of 4D reality. All our signs, symbols, emblems and words, however well chosen in attempts to point toward a 4D condition, are inherently formulated to express 3D realities. For language to be within the 4D condition, language itself must become energy. Language as energy is no more or less than rhythm, or tone. Music and poetic languages approach 4D energy realms more than other forms of language. Perhaps bird songs, wolf songs, dolphin songs, water falls, hot rocks steaming in a sweat lodge, are closer to 4D language than the words of most human language.

Our total human energy sensing capacities can move within a 4D space-time continuum realm where all is energy and all is sensed. The second we conceptualize that sensing we tend to loose 4D being-in-there-ness. (Unless we receive training in how to continue in 4D realms and form memory of those events.) Pagan cultures exert considerable effort in teaching the skills of receiving and incorporating experiences outside 3D realities. Learning to catch dreams is a very important entry to beginning to move our Energy-bodies in the realms of more than the commonly accepted world of industrial reality.

Energy blockages either intentionally or unintentionally placed in the 3D material world are more pervasive than we normally consider them to be. A dam constructed for hydroelectric power, irrigation, flood control and recreation may seem a good and practical human effort in industrial reality. However, the energy of that dammed-up river has suffered severe limitation. That energy interacted with rocks trees, oceans, 'wildlife' in wholly other rhythms before humans interfered. The ramifications of such a huge energy change are felt everywhere on earth. Viewed in the light of the principles of correspondence, dammed rivers have energy linkage with blocked veins in humans, the same humans who are part of the culture that constructs dams. Tendencies toward obesity are more pronounced in modern, industrial cultures where dams provide material energy and controlled water, helping to generate, not just power, but the conditions that foster obesity.

To function in 4D realities the limits of industrial culture must be overpowered. This does not mean that industrial culture must go away in order for that to happen. It means that a human instrument fully energized in 4D realms is able to step through, penetrate, totally incorporate experience while moving beyond 3D limits. Fourth dimension beings are different from those trapped within the material world. Their total energy is interactive, bright when observed, is much more than energies functioning as if 3D realities constituted all that is or could be.

The various blockages, that impose limits that keep us functioning only in 3D realities, become one with human physical, psychological bodies. It takes concentrated effort to overpower those limits. Physical body work by others through massage techniques can begin the loosening process. Yoga, Tai Chi and deep meditation, or cultural variants of these techniques, can repair our body-instrument. Finally, total movement into 4D realms happens as a release. Some call it the Shaman's death. Some refer to it as a leap into the abyss. However the breakthrough is experienced, the result is total change. Movement as a 4D creature is quite different from movement as a 3D creature. Limitation is recognized but continually penetrated, absorbed and left behind. In fourth dimensional, energy-flowing realities all possibilities and probabilities are present as they 'become,' 'are,' and flow away. Likewise fourth dimensional human Energy-bodies continually 'become,' flow, merge and disappear. Limitation looms always as a possibility. From a 4D reality perspective, however, limitations like all else are energies. Their presence is easily fortified and just as easily dissipated.

DOES DIMENSIONAL ENERGY HAPPEN WITHOUT LIMITS?

Humans organize in order to understand. Some humans assume chaos reigns where human patterns of understanding are absent. The question is does energy organize itself? Are there patterns prior to human conception? Do we recognize these patterns, our understanding being a reflection of them?

Pagan cultures are based on recognitions of energy patterns different from those of human generation. All is energy. Life is recognizable because living beings radiate and reflect energy. In the largest sense, all the beings of the night sky, stars and planets different from earth, have their own energy intensities, beam unique patterns, which, when studied over time by humans, appear rhythmic—literally the music of the spheres. Some of these rhythms cycle, they demonstrate patterns that have occurrence over specific periods of time. Some of these energy patterns are recognized as being like those emitted by familiar beings on earth, animals, plants, rivers, etc. In 4D reality cosmic energy patterning is always happening. It is the grand scheme within which all other life takes place. For pagan cultures energy patterning not only "makes sense" rationally, it is also obvious that the universe continually beams order into our lives in ways that exceed human understanding. It is our purpose as humans to discover and reflect that ordering. Only within those continually creating energies do we fulfill our potentials.

Astrological systems are maps of how cosmic 4D energies are continually patterning, organizing, moving through all beings. These energy-time maps make little sense within the limits of 3D rational systems. Since they utilize culturally-based languages to communicate their timing measurements, they remain, in the end, mere 3D maps of 4D realities.

In the cosmic scheme a star like the sun emits all kinds of wave energies which impact planets, asteroids, the moon, and all beings within the sun's range. Some cultures sense that the sun which gives us life interacts with a greater body that is sun-like, in the sense that it creates even the outer planets, suns, galaxies, etc. This "central sun" is functioning beyond or outside of human 3D perception. Some cultures equate this central sun with *the creator* in the sense that there is a being greater than all other beings who is worthy of human worship. Our languages again limit our abilities at such theistic comprehension.

Whenever we conceive of four dimensional energy realities we do so with 3D spatial languages. For us, all energy is a function of some sort of body or some relationship of bodies. Bodies need not be solid. They may be made of gas. They can even be conceived as made of energy. Their shape or form is necessary, however, if humans are to recognize their beingness. Sometimes we humans talk as if the space between bodies, the emptiness, the dark is filled with energy. We call it ectoplasm or other names in our attempts to speak of the limitlessness between shapes or forms which define limit.

On earth the greater cosmic energy fields interact with energies closely related to all cellular life. Physical bodies are born into already existing energy patterns. Some of these are the interactive patterning of planets and suns. Some are interactive cycles of streams, trees, atmosphere and other long-lived earth beings. Some are human cultural patterns passed along for at least 50 thousand years. Some are cycles much more pervasive than human cycles, yet basically invisible to human eyes, even though they have existed as cellular Kin on this planet for over 4.6 billion years according to our attempts to measure. These are the basic life forms: Monera, Eubacteri, Archaebacteria. Protocitists and Fungi form a whole other set of limits and dimensional realities, some seen, some unseen.

All life-forms emit energy and transmit energy. Each life-form is a peculiar Energy-body. All Eubacteria vibrate or transmit energy in a similar range. Their shape, in an energy sense, is a function of how rapidly their Energy-body pulsates. A wolf emits very dissimilar oscillations. A tree is again very different from other beings in its transmissions. And humans have distinctly recognizable Energy-body forms. Soils and rocks are alive with basic life forms and mineral forms, each of which emits and transmits waves and fields of recognizable energy.

All of this energy action is taking place at basic life levels. All cells are made up of DNA (Desoxyriboneclaic Acids) formed in unique, identifiable patterns. These patterns are themselves representative of the energies emitted by the cell(s) and the rate at which cells transmit all surrounding energy oscillations. Cells that emit vibrational energies that are out of synchronization with greater patterns are not healthy, in the sense that they are not being what they are supposed to be in the greater scheme of energies. They are sick.

Energy-bodies, like the human body, interact in the fourth dimension, stimulating, wounding, infecting, even killing the Energy-body forms of others. Pagan cultures are *very* aware of the primary nature of Energy-body interactions. Training in recognition techniques; healing (strengthening or raising transmission and resistance levels); proper interaction; journeying or pilgrimages or quests; energy building ceremonies; rituals of personal, partnered, community and universal capacities are all an education in a fourth dimension world. Learning about the energy centers within the human body—how they whirl, move and can suffer blockage—is a daily practice within pagan cultures. Chakras have many names depending upon language and understanding. Prana (the spirit-energy breath) also has many names. The basic understanding is however the same. The physical world is much more than it appears. It is an illusion if it is recognized as the only reality. If it is recognized as a manifestation of interactive energies, then our daily world is a mirroring of how all life is doing at a fourth dimensional level. In other words, we can study the material world if we realize that it reflects for us other constantly changing realities.

A Catechism for the Children of De-Light

WHAT IS AN ENERGY-BODY?

Throughout the material universe positive and negative charges vibrate. These vibrations generate perceivable symmetry. They veer and become asymmetrical only to reform patterns that appear balanced from a human viewpoint.

Energy-bodies are forms of positive and negative charges held by a force something like a human focus or the patterns resulting from human intention and attention. Energy-bodies, in that they take shape, generate recognizable vibrational patterns. You know a particular individual because your total sensing capability feels that individual's peculiar energy field. It feels totally unlike any other energy field, even though there may be similarities.

We recognize a live Energy-body because of its generation of energy waves or patterns. Energy-bodies always generate and transmit. If an Energy-body becomes a whirlpool-like vortex and swirls into itself, it is possible to feel it sucked into its opposite, which is nonexistence. Energy-bodies are always alive, moving, interacting, becoming different from what is currently manifesting. Stasis is not part of the dimensional journey that is the life of an Energy-body.

Energy-bodies move in 4D reality. Time-Space is a continuum. Energy-matter are one. There is no linearity. Human 3D systems of law, morality, economics and other limitations are as though transparent to Energy-bodies. Even gravity has no hold on an Energy-body. As in dreams, humans, human Energy-bodies can appear and disappear right side up or up side down or sideways all at once. Placement of recognizable body parts can be random. Energy-body patterns remain recognizable because of vibrational quality, not because of visual disclosure.

Energy-bodies, while generating vibrational waves (which identify individual potential/formation) are also totally receptive, having the capability to vibrate/dance with any other Energy-body projection. The potential for unity, in any moment, between Energy-body forms is always present. In pagan cultures, stories of these mergings abound, such as winged horses that are part human being. As these unities between two transmitting Energy-bodies occur, the very basis of perceiving can also switch. It is possible for humans to 'become' wolves, bears, and other animals. We can become microbes or trees and sense the world from within those identifiable Energy-body forms. Pagan cultures make a lifelong process of learning how to shape-shift, become-other, stalk character, experience the whole of a multidimensional experience. We are always as children when we play as Total Energy-bodies moving in 4D realities. The experiences are generally De-lightfilled, although there are instances where 3D fears, greed and other limiting actions break through into 4D reality and fill that reality with terror. It is for protection from such terrifying experiences that training, ritual and ceremony with cultured people is necessary.

ARE ENERGY-BODIES VISIBLE?

Human beings who are trained to function in 4D realities can 'see' Energy-bodies. Physical 3D bodies appear as luminescent. Generating, projecting, transmitting energies appear as colored light. Sometimes the 3D physical, biological, chemical body appears transparent. Sometimes that body appears as solid with bands of energy around the body, shaped like an ever rounder bubble, in motion and with pastel to bright colors, like the northern lights.

Sometimes Energy-bodies have left 3D reality. Ghosts, spirits, apparitions, angels, monsters, trolls, fairies and a host of other beings exist and are perceptible within 4D multidimensional context. 'Seeing' these beings requires total 4D sensing of potential energy formation. Often only glimpses in his or her receptors hold the perception of the potential formation or shape. Pagan cultures teach how to receive and hold potential energy formations, how to interact with them so as not to have them instantly 'disappear' as recognition is established. The animal world, the plant world, the microbial world, water, air and fire all have Energy-body reflections in 4D realities and can manifest for human instruments if we are so attuned.

Energy-bodies are visible because they are recognizable. They emit shapes and vibratory tones familiar to us within 3D reality. We know a familiar 'dead' family member is around because we sense their presence vibrationally, usually before we see some aspect of them, if we see them at all. We know a teacher or angelic protecting being because they return to us over and over, establishing trusted vibratory relationship. Likewise we know when Energy-bodies that are unfamiliar are present. When such an occurrence happens we scan that body, sensing compatible tone or discord. Pagan cultures teach how to ward off discordant beings, beings that do not allow your particular Energy-body instrument to emit freely, ring fully, to function with full potential.

IS THERE A DIFFERENCE BETWEEN ENERGY-BODIES, SOULS AND SPIRITS?

Language limits are incurred when we speak of being within a 4D context. The language of Energy-bodies is an attempt to describe physical potentials that remain free flowing, unencumbered by words/names in languages that function dualistically. The use of the term 'Energy-body' to identify presences in vibration is a nod to Einstein's formulations, which seem to resonate with and amplify traditional pagan teachings worldwide.

The orthodoxies of the dominant culture separate the material world from the world of spirit. In earlier parts of this Catechism that dualism was discussed. Pagan cultures link 4D realities with the material world, inclusive of all beings on this planet, all life beyond this planet, on other planets, and outward to other stars and galaxies. Spirit is not separate from such life, but is one with it. For this reason, the orthodoxy dismisses pagan understandings as pantheistic. For them, God creates 3D reality, but is not of it. Spirit participates within 3D reality but 3D reality does not itself exude spirit. These are crucial differences.

The idea of Soul is closer to that of Energy-bodies, but again it is a concept that reflects dualism. A human soul (in most orthodox interpretations animals, rocks and trees do not have souls) is a meeting place for the outside spiritual world and the material world body. Soul connotes depth, the third dimension in a two dimensional dualistic conception of the universe. Soul, however, functions within acceptable limits, its communications— vibration, emotion, one's vital essence being shared—limited as well. That communication is not free in the sense that all vibrational interchange is a possibility. It is within the 3D moment, not in 4D space-time, energy-matter continuum.

Ultimately the use of the term *Energy-bodies*, to identify potential living formations, is dimensionally different from the use of either the words soul or spirit. The Energy-body as vibrational instrument is quite a different conception from the material body containing a soul or being in contact with spirit.

WHERE DO ENERGY-BODIES COME FROM?

Energy-bodies manifest as potential form or shape when two energies become one. In other words, Energy-bodies are the results of relationships of generating energies. An Energy-body is an energy birth that has taken shape in a direction that is recognizable in that it reflects a form or shape that could be seen within the material world 3D reality.

In the view of post quantum theory, relativity astronomers and physicists, there was a beginning to energy birth in a big Bang 20-50 billion years ago. All other births are an effect of the universe cooling and expanding. Free energy slows down as it cools to become matter. What if some energies continue to function at faster than matter rates? What if whole realms or dimensions of realities pulse and vibrate as the results of breaking tensions that exist beside, but outside of, reality as we know it in material sense? Physicists speak of the great heat involved in atomic and sub-atomic collisions, fracturing, breaking apart, allowing for creations. But these creations are only of matter. What if within those collisions, and all collisions of energy-matter, other forms of energy are simultaneously at work? What kind of forces bring about the symmetry that is everywhere apparent? Is what we see as beauty a universal force, a tendency to shape in which brain waves generated by this force, translate nerve tensions into patterns? When a positive and a negative force collide, male and female, a tension is formed, a dynamic that will eventually snap, breaking the original beings and forming at least one new being. The nature of this 'beingness' is like the essence that is referred to by all the various conceptual names ever used, gathered all at once. Beingness is matter-energy, mind-spirit, space-time, hence a sensation we humans often feel as De-Light.

Energy-bodies do not just form and sit there. Energy-bodies are in continual flux. Their formation is linked to a relationship with energy-matter bodies. Energy-bodies can and do exist apart from energy-matter, but they are only recognizable in relation to energy-matter forms or beings. *Energy-bodies require a force like intention or attention to shape themselves.* When humans apply intention or attention to energy-body-shaping it is possible to shape-shift, to change not only the look but the vibrational tone of the Energy-body. Beings that have a looser relationship with material plane 3D reality choose to appear/vibrate in whatever manner is necessary for a receptor to recognize them.

Individual beings are collections of both positive and negative, male and female energy tendencies, shaped in a set of tensions in space-time. The energy interactions within that tension generate recognizable color, presence and shape for, what we call, the Energy-body. *Energy-bodies are projections of relationships happening within a set of tensions.*

This dynamic is so basic that we celebrate it in ritual, liturgy, and drama. We reenact the creation of tension and the breaking of that tension which has the effect of shape-shifting, changing the vibratory presence of all those involved, including those who think of themselves as observers.

ARE THERE PHANTOM ENERGY-BODIES?

Energy-bodies are alive. We know this as we sense their presence as one which is continually pulsing, ever shining outward, like a fairy or candle light. However, when one is function-ing in 4D realities you might be fooled by 'dead' projections, images that exist not because they are generating life, but images that are distractions, intentionally or unintentionally hurled into our sensing. How do we recognize such dimensional tricks?

Sometimes those shapes or forms feel flat, don't even have a sense of 3D life. These are easily rejected, if you are alert. What is more disturbing is to encounter images, shapes, whole vibratory relationships that appear alive but are not. Often these false beings are mental projections sent into 4D reality by someone whose intent is to disrupt, as might a black magician. As long as your own Energy-body is vital, functioning at high tension alert-ness, projecting all the transmissions your instrument is capable of emitting, then a dead or false Energy-body will bounce off your life form. Distractions will not displace you from being who you are, in your totality. However, if you allow your Energy-body to weaken, turn in on itself, then the energy of distraction can seem attractive, seem life-giving, can in fact divert you from your possibilities of becoming.

Media tools like television have the capability of overpower-ing Energy-bodies with distraction. The high-tech corporate world culture uses these energies to mesmerize, in effect turning generating Energy-bodies into mere receptors. For an alert human individual the experience is humiliating. It is a gross violation, a rape. Yet for the masses of people caught up in popu-lar consumer culture such major dead-image distractions are their link to life. Without them, they feel lost, empty, without direc-tion. So great is the power of entertainment, amusement, news, and the all-pervasive messages of popular music, that this pro-jected unreality seems a fuller reality than life without these false projections. Blocking the influence of non-life images requires conscious removal of attention to their invasive force. This usually requires removing yourself to remote, non-urbanized places. But for those raised with mass media as culture, it can be frightening to be alone high in the mountains with only the wind and the wolves and birds. For most people regaining a presence with our total human instrument is little more than a remote wish.

Phantom Energy-bodies do not actually emit energy. They may appear as if they emit, but that is only as part of a context, such as exists in the viewer's relationship to TV, movies or the internet, which keep a perceiver in the role of observer rather than participant. You know when you are in relationship with a non-life-energy-body-image because you watch, you do not interact. Two do not become one. There is no birthing resulting from the meeting.

ARE ENERGY-BODIES VULNERABLE TO OTHER DISTURBANCES?

Your Total Energy-body sensing instrument can be 'injured' by violence, accident, psychic anger attack, sudden loud noise, subtle and persistent background noise, color, motion, rhythm, smell or interaction with another Energy-body that is weakened in some way. You are also weakened by directed and residual wave energies like microwave radiation. (In fact many governments now use directed energy weapons.) Energy-body resilience requires daily maintenance. Meditation, Tai Chi, yoga, and other forms of dimensional energy expansion-work keeps Energy-body bubbles healthy in humans. Being in an area with fresh air, or with trees in forests, or near a stream or ocean, or with animals in natural habitat, all are environments that can allow for the fullness of the 4D Energy-body. The energy forms of these other beings rooted in place, flowing in a place, or interaction with other life forms, free of human interference or limitation, are supportive in a inter-active sense of our Energy-body possibilities.

When Energy-bodies are injured they shrink or crack. Some-times only portions of an Energy-body are struck, causing that portion to dent. Sometimes whole Energy-bodies are shrunken, usually by prolonged subtle overpowering interferences such as television, an overpowering parent or other authority, or some sort of imprisoning physical or psychological condition, such as a bad marriage or other relationship which one feels forced to endure. Intense, prolonged fear shrinks free-flowing Energy-bodies.

Humans, other animals, plants, fungi, algae, microorganisms are more susceptible to disease when their Energy-bodies are not fully flowered—when they are constricted or shrunken. Sometimes the effects of an Energy-body assault are almost immediate, within hours or days. If this is sufficiently severe it may require a strong influx of Energy-body 'healing' to weather or survive a condition. Often several months pass before the effects of the attack manifest in the material body. Once one recognizes that the physical, biological body is sick because of a prior energy event, the recognition itself triggers the healing. A death in the family or car accident or some other severe shock may not pass through the Energy-body into physical manifestation until six months later. By then we often don't associate such an earlier event with a current condition. But when we do, we notice a sudden relief, a rebuilding of strength.

Gardeners can see plant vitality suddenly overpowered by a caretaker whose personal energy field is angry or depressed. Or, on the other hand, like Japanese gardeners whose Energy-bodies are maintained with meditation and ceremony, a gardener can touch plants an give them more vitality than they already have. Healing energy is a shared, vital, fully flowing Energy-body interaction. Humans, all living things, interact in the same way.

HOW DO ENERGY-BODIES INTERACT?

Energy-bodies move in at least four dimensional reality. Energy-body activity, like all 4D motion, is much faster than that of 3D reality. Your fully activated Energy-body is capable of fantastic feats. A fully activated Energy-body can appear and be perceived in more than two places, simultaneously. An Energy-body can merge with another Energy-body in a more total feeling of union than sexual union without being in actual proximity with the other.

Energy-body interactions in hyperspace (multidimensional) display forms that 'appear' as moving particles or segments of particles. An Energy-body looks like billions of fragments, each once pulsing within a field. When two Energy-bodies interact at a distance, the pulsing is stimulated, changing vibration as a result of the interaction. When two Energy-bodies interact in proximity, there is slippage, particle fragments merging with other particle fragments, forming a shape different from either of the two shapes that are interacting. Energy-body merging creates other Energy-body forms, which in turn relate with the two Energy-bodies that originally formed. All beings relate in this way if they are allowed to, if there is not too much interference from clusters of energy that distract or block natural flow.

Interaction between Energy-bodies requires more than attraction. When one Energy-body is attracted to another it may move into the zone of the energy field of the Energy-body to which attraction occurs, but remaining in that field, or merging with that field, *requires a dynamic like intention*. This dynamic is not specifically psychological, although in human understanding that is how we can best express in words the focus-attention-aim necessary for attraction and interaction to happen. Intention energy seems a limited language concept when we shift our examples to plants and insects or other beings. A weak plant sends out a different form of energy than a healthy plant. Certain insects attuned to plant energy patterns hone-in-on weaker plants, merge energies with the plant, and physically devour them, changing plant energy into insect energy in the process. There may be birds in the area attuned to insect energies. From seemingly nowhere a entire flock of birds may appear simply because of the presence of insects attuned to weak plants. These birds may in turn devour many or all of the insects, then disappear, not to be observed in that area again. Some birds are attuned to very specific plant vibrational energies. I observed a bird who does not normally live anywhere near our area appear one summer to sing in a field planted with a grain that has not been grown in this local. When the grain was harvested the bird disappeared. That particular grain was not planted again. The bird, from an area where this grain is a more common crop, has not returned. Such attractions of life forms for one another seem to defy any sense of linear distance, time, or normal pattern. Humans, interacting dimensionally, may live thousands of miles apart, may even live in what appear as different linear time periods, yet their interaction at a Total Energy-body level can be more intense, total and consuming than any relationship that involves only physical/psychological 3D realities or sporadic 4D interactions.

WHAT EXISTS IN AN ENERGY-BODY FIELD?

When we are our Total Energy-body reality in a 4D sense we are much more complex, in a immediate sense, than we appear in 3D reality. We are all the manifestations of self that we have ever been, in various 3D realities, in various linear times. We are 'selves' we have been in 4D and other dimensional realities. Recognition of another Energy-body often feels extremely powerful, more than 3D reality allows. That is because with higher pulsation, in 4D dimensional realities, attraction is not limited by space-time or by the energy constraints of matter. The 4D 'space' allows us to unfold into our total complexity to be immediately and simultaneously 'there.'

One example, of simply not sensing or interacting with the full complexity of perception available to our Energy-body, happens between humans all the time. We are physically attracted. We express that physical attraction over time with affection and sexual interaction. Then one day we realize that this other person is not who we thought they were. They begin to seem to have all kinds of characteristics that have no discernible basis in the person we thought we knew. Some of this may be accounted for as we learn of their physical history in this life, of family, previous relationships, how they learned, sickness, basis for fear, etc. But there is always more. We learn, if we take the time to learn, that the totality of this other person is vast, that it spans lifetimes and lifetimes as well as all kinds of pervious total energy mergings.

If two Energy-body fields are open enough to explore all that is carried in their collective Energy-body fields, it can take a lifetime, in the chronological sense. Such an exploration might then be an exploration of many cultures, many time periods, of a huge 'family' of energy relationships that are every bit as real as any 'blood' relationship in the current 3D life.

Pagan cultures encourage Total Energy-body interaction, recognition, exploration. Certain people consistently emerge who can see Energy-body complexity and act from the basis of this capacity for the benefit of others. Such seers are highly revered. They are consulted and their insights are taken into account when deliberations and decisions are being made. Relegating these seers to positions of misfits, quacks, outsiders, insane people, as is routinely done in modern industrial-technological orthodoxies, or has been done by the church-mosque-temple traditions, is to admit that one does not function in 4D and other realities. It is to deny the importance of dimensional information, which informs us in a much more complex and complete way than limited 3D science or pseudo science or 'history' or other disciplines.

HOW DO WE MOVE DIMENSIONALLY?

Dimensional motion in higher- or faster-than-3D reality requires of humans that we focus, that we use the forces equated with the feeling of intention. We must 'close-out' interference. This often requires setting up energy safe zones, through ritual, ceremony, or limiting of the use of a space. Sometimes a safe zone can be found in nature, as on a remote mountain or in a wood or meadow where 3D reality fades and totality of presence takes over.

The experience of moving into the 4th Dimension and beyond frequently feels like entering a tunnel at very high speed, a tunnel which is often described as being of golden light. Physicists who derive dimensions mathematically theorize a concept called 'tunneling.' The experience of pagan peoples who move dimensionally is always one of moving quickly beyond the limits and confines of 3D worlds, flashing into parallel realities, which 'look like' 3D realities, but where as individuals we move very close to the speed of light, without confines of forces like gravity and non-penetrable matter.

Colors in these realities are 'brighter,' sometimes having an almost crystalline quality. Motion is effortless, the effort being more like what we usually recognize as psychological forces, intention, attention, focus. Meetings with other entities can be very different from 3D reality. Entities 'take the form of' shapes or energies that human consciousness can recognize. Then they might shape shift into wholly other forms, some of which we recognize, some of which we don't. Entities living within other dimensions are often characterized with anthropomorphic (human characteristic or form) bodies. Their voices or communications are like voices we 'hear' or 'see' and can therefore understand. Yet their own energy shapes and communication devices may be nearer to what we perceive as non-form, pure non-material or faster than 3D material energy fields.

All of the principles considered in this catechism allow us to understand experiences within 4D and other dimensional realities, but only if we let the energies emitted by other dimensional entities and circumstances transmute into forms which we can understand in a 3D way. We are capable of being and communicating at higher dimensional levels, but our attempts at interpreting that beingness bring us back to 3D reality and its limitations of language and material form. These transmutations take practice and training. One of the reasons pagan cultures have a resilience that conquering 3D 'cultures' have not been able to crush is that pagan cultures function multi-dimensionally, since much of the information and essence of understanding is passed generation to generation through higher dimension Total Energy-body communications. We are not limited by death in a 3D sense. Nor are we limited by burning of libraries, or outlawing of rituals and ceremonies as the dominant culture has routinely done over the centuries.

A Catechism for the Children of De-Light

HOW DO MASTERS WORK WITH HUMANS AND HUMAN HISTORY?

In 4D and higher dimensions, entities live without time as a constraint. Those of us who have chosen to enter 3D reality, to live with limit and learn the lessons of material reality, can also live interactively with entities in other dimensions. One of the limits imposed by being birthed on earth is that 'perceptual doors' are closed, unless they are intentionally kept open by appropriate cultural and personal activity based on awareness of other dimensions. We forget who we are in an Energy-body sense. We don't remember the 'all' that we are, or who is all around us dimensionally. Pagan cultures teach techniques for staying in contact with entities that inhabit other dimensions. Because these entities are outside 3D reality they can often advise those of us who live within 3D reality how to navigate limitation. We often equate the advice and counsel of these entities with 'wise ones' on earth, white hairs, older humans whose long lives and often whose dimensional relationships are recognized as superior to advice or counsel from those caught within limit, no matter how high the intellectual level attained. When these dimensional beings come to us they are often given names, characteristics we can recognize, making use of 3D languages to express 4D and other dimensional communications. In Western cultures the term 'Master' has been applied to those who teach dimensionally. Master teachers from other dimensions speak through mediums or instruments living within 3D planes. Priests and other teachers in both pagan and dominant cultures are, by formal definition of their role, open for dimensional communications. In preparation their physical-bio-logical-psychological instruments are trained and with practice they can be attuned to receive or interact in an Energy-body totality.

CAN WE BECOME OTHER BEINGS?

Pagan cultures spend much time and energy creating and performing ceremony and ritual. Usually these events coincide with cosmic events, of great significance for earth life, such as the fullness or newness of the moon or winter and summer solstices of the sun. During these ceremonies or during individual vision quests or other 'hunting' preparations (hunting or seeking when done dimensionally, as interactions with other Energy-bodies, are more than those words suggest to us in our ordinary understanding) pagan cultures teach the participant how to become 'other,' a merging with Energy-bodies not limited to our own species. It is possible for us to 'become' another being, enter into that other—animal, tree or microbe—thereby partaking of its way of perceiving and of moving. The 'medicine' ways of the natives of Asia, the Americas, the Pacific islands, and the early Europeans, were and are, lessons in learning limits of other earth beings while we are here in physical and Energy-body form. Shape shifting, transmutation of Energy-body into totally 'other,' stalking a character until you become that character, as well as preserving your totally complex human form, these are all possibilities for cultures which teach how to move with intention in more than the familiar dimension.

Dimensional energy or Total Energy-body interrelation is closer to our understanding of electromagnetic energy than any other we perceive, at least in our language at this time. Dimensional energy fields are symbolized by fire. Fire is like the sun. Fire is like ionization. Fire is like all dimensional motion, which is felt as heat-producing, light-giving.

Fire is usually the center of the ceremonies, rituals and symbology in pagan cultures. In many stories fire is given or stolen from other worlds. These stories allow us to tell how dimensional energy works, how it is experienced in the telling as De-Light, generation after generation during all the seasons of Earth.

A Catechism for the Children of De-Light

Awareness in decision-making based on Part IX

1. We sense our limits.
2. Training and intention can open us to at least four dimensions.
3. Energy interaction happens universally.
4. Total Energy-body awareness brings De-Light..
5. Total Energy-body interactions allow us to move dimensionally.

PART X
PRINCIPLES OF
RELATIONSHIP

A Catechism for the Children of De-Light

WHO ARE 'ALL OUR RELATIONS'?

Relationship allows De-Light to manifest most easily. Our individual sense of more-than-oneness is either a catalyst to stimulate our Total Energy-body awareness creatively outward so we can share, or an excuse for us to set up defenses in fear of all those other entities out there, seeing them as a threat. In a free-flowing energy 4D reality you must choose how you interact, moment to moment, in all dimensions. You must choose when to flow and when to hold. And you must be ready to take the instantaneous consequences of either choice. If you choose to hold back free flowing creativeness, your world becomes one of imposed limits or walls, a fortress under attack or ready to counterattack.

Native cultures pray for ALL our relations. Modern Biochemistry has allowed us to appreciate the complexity of all these relations, to extend our understanding of who they are and how we are related. All our relations in 3D reality begin with the amazing web of simple life forms here on this planet: Monera, Eubacteria, Archebacteria, Protocitists and Fungi. For something like 4.6 billion years (by human reckoning) these mostly unseen, webs of life forms, have generated and regenerated on this planet. They are our most precious relations. Without them, life as we know it would not exist. But they too have even more primary relationships. Minerals, or earth, water—the union of hydrogen and oxygen gases—and air or atmosphere—made up of very delicate balance of primary universal gases—are our relations. Without all the relationships of molecular, ionic and atomic structuring and unstructuring, occurring moment to moment everywhere in dimensional reality, life would also not exist. One of our mutual, primary relations is fire, explosion, light, the event that happens each time a Total Energy-body of any 'being,' any relation, merges, transmutes or transforms, as it moves freely toward relationship with another 'being.' All our relations are not just the animals and trees, the grasses and mountains or all the natural beauty we perceive in 3D reality, if we are bothering to look at all. All our relations are ALL, all life in the universe, including the most basic molecules of gases, many of which we, as humans, may not yet be aware of. Plants and animals are closer to human life forms, so we tend to think only of them when we pray, when we make decisions as to how we live. However, all the plants and animals including humans are minuscule when we consider the abundance of any of several thousand kinds of already identified bacteria. Other such life forms are far more populous inhabitants of this universe than we typically consider. All are alive, vibrating! These are Total Energy-body forms with which we interact, forming relationships, whether we are aware of them or not.

HOW DO WE RELATE?

We are all Kin in multiple ways. Life forms on this planet share an ancestry through common DNA (desoxynucleaic acid). This bio-information makes humans relations, in a biological sense, with all animals and birds and sea creatures, and with worms and bugs and bacteria. Many native peoples speak of crystalline relationship, meaning that we share electrolytes (minerals) and chemical structures with all creatures and with all rocks, soils, with particles of any kind. We are all energy-matter relations, all positive-negative ions in tension-vibration. In short, we are all Total Energy-bodies, very much alike but in recognizably different forms.

The fallacy of humanism or anthropomorphism is that it makes humans the constant center of millions of non-human relationships. Humans are 'like' but still very unlike other beings. To appreciate our relatedness to all other life forms we must appreciate our human totality, Total Energy-bodyness, but we must realize and revere all other forms of total energy. We are not 'better' than other life forms, nor are we more complete, or more complex, nor are we 'higher' life forms. We are a life form with incredible capacity to freely relate with all other life forms. However, if we try to dominate, manipulate and control, then we set up limitations, we stop energy flow and we generate anti-life.

A Catechism for the Children of De-Light

HOW DO WE COMMUNICATE WITH ALL OUR RELATIONS?

We humans are each individual ones. We are also a species, a collective energy. As individual ones we are identifiable as Total Energy-bodies. From a multidimensional perspective our identity is recognizable as forming fields of colored light, a peculiar bubble shape. Within that form swirling patterns or centers that appear as generating lights reveal intensity and gender. We each carry a unique energy body identity.

Often our Energy-body is out of balance. The form may appear skewed, twisted, unable to flow, even dark. Often physical gender characteristics dominate the energy patterning; we are either predominately feminine or masculine. In the dimensional world of Total Energy-bodies we seek balance, for we sense that balance as health. Intuitively, we seek union, usually of male and female, and on earth we seek or are drawn to our other half in a reflection through another person, a separate Total Energy-body. To be a Total Energy-body we need be both male and female. Ultimately, that sexual positive-negative balance must happen within our own being. It cannot happen except as teaching in a symbolic way between two incomplete Energy-bodies. As humans mature, much of the ripening or wisdom we gain, manifests as vibrational balancing—a physical woman expressing more of her masculine side, a man expressing more of his feminine side. Total vibrational sharing allows for all this change, growth, expression of totalness. We are probably never fully balanced, but if balance is encouraged, nurtured, promoted, then we are more likely to be receptive of balanced complexity.

The modern dominant culture, world wide, sells imbalance, promotes unbalanced Energy-bodies, wounded energies based in fear. Consider musical lyrics. Watch the videos and movies. Carefully observe advertising. Possession and loss of another, usually in a male-female context, is the dominant theme of the dominant culture. Bombarded by this scenario we then project our incompleteness onto another, despite the impossibility of that longing being filled in this manner. We are not prodded daily to develop our Total Energy Beings, at least that does not happen within the dominant culture's institutions and marketing schemes. Instead we are encouraged to treat another Energy-body as property. Relationship as ownership sets up all kinds of limitations, reducing the creative-generating-energy necessary for the daily sensing of De-Light.

Other Energy-bodies different from our own can teach us about our own capacities and abilities. They can reflect difference for us. But they cannot be a substitute for our own completeness. Until we mature enough to come into harmony with all or most of our positive and negative, male-female paradoxical potential, we cannot feel Total Energy-body free flow. Only an individual human can achieve human balance. No one can do it for her/him. It takes attention and intent to become what we are on earth to be. Otherwise we are continually chasing distractions.

Many would argue that we must maintain a difference between our civic being and our private total energy being. This split causes modern humans to act as though we are schizophrenic, our daily lives not open to free flowing energies. This sham is a sign that daily life is misdirected from a total energy standpoint. It is a warning that to feel De-Light we might have to step away from conventional modern 3D reality expectations.

Communications between Total Energy-bodies happen as vibratory sensation. You feel, you sense, the presence of another. There is not necessarily any need for other forms of language, except as a longing to express a sense of recognition that total two-becoming-oneness has happened, IS happening. Total Energy-body sensing is primal, pre-language, or more than language. You just 'know.'

This kind of communication can take place between creatures of the same species, like two humans. It can take place between humans and other animals, with plants, with unseen microbes, with entities of other dimensions, with crystalline forms, with all life generating presences. Total presence does not require special proximity. Communication can take place between two Energy-bodies seemingly separated by thousands of miles and many generations.

Total Energy-body communication often happens between non equals. The most common occurrence is between humans and animals, from a human perspective. Two humans, dissimilar in age, sex, language, occupation, interests might also experience Total Energy-body communication. Humans and plants, especially garden or house plants are often in total relationship with each other.

For total communication to take place both parties must be non-defensive. Humans characterize the vibratory tone of such a situation as one of trust. Both parties are simultaneously in a state of total reception and total giving. There is a sense of excitement, stimulation, creative potential in the moment. Once mutual presence is established there is an overwhelming feeling of unity or oneness, sometimes described as an energy bubble. From the outside looking at Total Energy-body wave patterns, colors mix, tiny energy fragments dance, polarities of two Energy-bodies interspersed with waves of creative tension hover, poised in union. In a 4D space-time continuum Total Energy-body communication may last an instant or forever. There is no linear measurement to this union. When linearity enters, the vibratory moment shifts from one of free flowing trust to one of control, wanting to hang on, wanting to savor, trying to possess either the feeling of the moment or the other Energy-body involved in the union. Humans often describe the dimensional sensations of Total Energy-body communication as Love. The meanings of love are many, and more often than not involve linear interpretations of a other-than-total energy kind.

Limitations are formed by the need to use the other being, to project one's own Energy-body upon that other being, to own, to rely on—all connotations associated with human love. Negative polarities within the 'love' state such as jealousy, hate, envy, depression over loss, are all extensions of limitations associated with love that are not really Total Energy-body communication.

A Catechism for the Children of De-Light

Sometimes beings meet and experience Total Energy-body communication of a very complete kind, then never meet again in 3D earth reality. They may continue meeting in 4D or other dimensional realms, simultaneously with a 3D earth life. Some of these meetings may be remembered as private or shared stories, more important to understanding an incarnation than the experiences of and the situations that occur within, a linear, day-in and day-out, framework.

When two or more Total Energy-bodies communicate fully, a merger takes place. Such creative unification requires both, or all, Total Energy-bodies involved to be in agreement. We are individual instruments through which continual evolving, dissipating and revolving, creative energies move. We are De-Light. To come into agreement our individual instruments must be totally accepting of this process. Like a duet or an orchestra, our vibratory life must be moving toward harmonies, or even intended discords. We must be receptive to the overall purpose that we are life-bringers, Light promoters, vessels of a process which we can totally sense, but which goes on continually with or without our particular presence.

When two Total Energy-bodies or a group of Total Energy-bodies struggle to allow themselves to be formed-receptacles that are themselves totally flowing energy patterns, then the potential for 4D interactive realities within a 3D world exists. In the best of situations pagan assemblies or councils were, and are formed, in this manner. Many different perceivings, sexes, ages, species, visible and non-visible entities are called to make decisions regarding how 3D life is to be lived in a interactive 4D manner.

Energy-body instruments aligned in agreement shift individual forms to become the greater Total Energy-body, to act in agreement as one. They shape-shift. While maintaining recognizable individual centers, absorption of another presence changes the total energy context in which agreement is taking place. The ability to shape shift is a central teaching of all pagan cultures. Without the ability to become other, for whatever reason, total energy communication is not possible. It might be necessary for a human or group of humans to become a fish, for instance, in order to communicate with fish in an open energy council to decide why fish are disappearing and what would allow them to return. In human hunting societies Total Energy-body communication skills were essential. In the industrialized market-based cultures which dominate humans today, we tend to think these skills unnecessary, even dangerous, and some would say demonic or perverted. Yet, without Total Energy-body communication skills and awareness we have no place among all the life beings of this and other universes.

HOW DO WE COMMUNE WITH ENTITIES DIFFERENT FROM OURSELVES?

Hunting and agricultural cultures recognize the importance of cross species communication in a Total Energy-body sense. Many of the clans and societies within these cultures specialize in a particular kind of communion with a particular or narrow range of species. The Eagle clan carries out its teachings quite differently, and yet similarly, from the Wolf clan or the Bear clan. How each of the members of these clans is taught to interact with plant, insect, fungi and other creatures is dependent upon the methods used to establish Total Energy-body interaction by the creature whose perceiving is most revered by that clan. In many pagan cultures it is understood that humans are born as reflections; reflections of star and planetary alignments at the time of first breath, reflections of one or more animal or bird or reptile or insect or other creature perceiving at birth, reflections of the condition of the mother during gestation, as she reflects the condition of our earthly mother. We are carriers of the 'perceivings' of other life, of bloodlines on this planet. We are reflections of ALL our relations. We are very complex Total Energy-bodies with incredible potential to interact with all other Total Energy-bodies, which are equally complex.

To communicate with our own complexities and the complexities of others requires focused action. Communion/communication is ceremony. It is ritual. Total communication requires that one individual become total, then merge that totality with another who has become total. Often this process is done with use of physical parts of the other, such as feathers, furs, hides, claws, teeth, or in the case of plants, seeds or pollen or dried leaves. Sometimes masks, mirroring a creatures essence, are used to facilitate communion. Motions, how a being moves, are learned and mimicked in dance.

Communication with angels, devas, fairies, teachers and guides from other dimensions requires a similar attention-merging. To achieve total communion with other dimensional beings, images are evoked, names are spoken, offerings are given.

The purpose of Total Energy-body communion/communication is not replication. It is not repetition. Often such communion happens in the same way only once. What occurs in these communions is learning, expansion, exploration of potential, in the individual, in the group, and between entities. Total communion, or even attempting total communion, is open sharing, is the sensation of De-light.

Total human communication requires equally complex attention, focus, total energy merging. It requires appreciation that the other human or humans involved in the communion are different, therefore sharing from a different, exciting, complexly unique perception or perspective. 'Stalking' a character is a way of stating the practice of so appreciating or revering another being that you are able to merge with them, see, sense, from their totalness.

Some entities vibrate at more intense energies than others. Children, for instance, are delicate energy fields which can be "burned" by a being with a very developed energy field who is allowing too much of that field to interact with the child's field. We must be so aware of the other that we merge in total ways that do not overpower, but have the effect of empowering. Pagan cultures teach the slow development of personal energy fields, of bodies. As individuals we can only take-on so much of a faster or more intense vibration at any one interaction. However, like capacitors or resisters, our Total Energy-body can handle increasing vibratory load as we interact with entities of more intense vibration. The mechanical/technological "noise" of contemporary dominant cultures can be so intense as to form a disruptive shield so that Total Energy-bodies cannot recognize each other, cannot easily interact. Three-dimensional reality can get a person conditioned to replication, repetition, comfort associated with pleasure and ease, thereby retreating into versions of the material body that are not super-sensitized, alert and focused with intent to seek and learn—ready for total merging.

Sharing with white hairs, elders, and entities of other dimensions that have more Total Energy-body experience than we have is a way to learn potential. Stories of their experiences, while not repeatable, take us beyond our knowledge learned in life this time or other times on earth. If we truly share in the communion of these experiences, we take on those experiences as stalkers, not as observers. In fact, a role for science in a Total Energy-body sense, is for scientific investigators to become what they are looking at, to be stalkers rather than observers. Like the hunters in older cultures, stalking microorganisms in a microscope, or participating in collisions of subatomic particles and studying their traces, could/should be performed as ceremony, ritual, with opening prayers, thanksgiving, and closing benediction, completeness, thanks for the revelation of how energy-matter entities move, commune, be.

The communion most often entered into by humans and other animals and sexual entities is male-female sharing. Sex is so important because it is how in 3D reality we tend to perceive the extension of ourselves into another unlike ourselves. For total merging to happen, total focus and total attention to Total Energy-bodies merging must happen. Some pagan cultures view human sexual interaction as a, or the, primary way to learn total energy sharing. Sex can be an opening for Total Energy-body interaction, if the people or other entities involved focus that way. However, more often, sex is not continually expansive. It is repetitive. What can be experienced in deep sexual sharing is pure De-Light, creative generation, the feeling of potential that is possible in all moments of life. For this to happen two sexual partners must be equally attentive to total energies associated with physical intercourse. There is no body separate from the Total Energy-body, yet we often pretend and act as if there were. When we do celebrate the total potential of intercourse the energy bubble created stays with us as individuals for hours, even days. Energy invigoration of more intense vibration allows us to feel more total, therefore to share more easily with many other Total Energy-bodies.

WHAT IS POWER?

Power is the focusing of the Total Energy-body emissions. Power does not happen in isolation. It is always a function of the interaction of two or more Total Energy-bodies.

The power emitted by a stallion, running at the lead of a wild herd, is awesome to behold. What is coming through that horse as 'instrument' is not only all the possibility of his muscle, nerve, horse-ness, it is his intent to set direction, to emit strength that can be shared with all the horses in that herd.

Power coming through a trained human Total Energy Being, a shaman, is equally awesome. Energies from all kinds of interactive energy relationships are continually received, transmitted, transmuted and emitted in a manner focused for whatever the intent of the moment requires. Using breath, voice and body as vehicles all aspects of the human energy potential are enacted: electromagnetic types of wave energies are moved and radiated outward, for the healing attunement of the 3D world with all other dimensions of reality.

Power is a result of relationship with other Total Energy-bodies emitting at very intense levels, often beyond human perception abilities. We are continually surrounded by entities radiating focused power that is available for our total interaction. Human or human-like personages such as angels, guides, people who have "died," all are available for Total Energy-body council. Unseen entities of a biological and subatomic nature, with their unique 'offerings,' are also available for us. We are never alone. We are within a gigantic Total Energy-body life-pulsation, which feeds and fills our Energy-body instrument as long as it accepts and transmits freely.

Power can be transmitted or transmuted for the purpose to turn or de-focus other living entities. Teachers, guides, healers utilize the energy coming through them to overpower Total Energy-bodies whose vibrations are wounded, less intense, disruptive, or not able to be totally flowing in a creative, generative, manner.

Overpowering is a delicate procedure. It requires that the human or other Total Energy-body instrument through which possibly immense surges of cosmic energy flow are transmitted, to be unattached to both the energy and the results of the energy direction. In other words, if you are in the role of healer to a wounded person, you must be a channel for healing energy, and when the channeling is no longer required, you must be free for the next level of energy transmission, whatever that may be. The same is true for teaching or guiding. Directed energy flow can accomplish amazing changes within 3D reality if we allow that flow, without our interference. Each occurrence of Total Energy-body relationship is a kind of test in which we are allowing what *needs* to happen as opposed to what we may *want* to happen. It is very easy to be distracted, allowing an open, free flowing Total Energy-body to slip into some form of limitation, thereby restricting potential. Often such distraction is an urge to possess or control the moment, either the situation, or the other entity.

Directed power should empower! It should strengthen the instrument through which it passes. It should result in the object of the energy transmission being more vital, filled with potential and possibility that comes from that entity's energy center(s). A person acting in Total Energy-body mode, allowing power to move through her/him, will feel De-Light as you recognize another Energy-body being empowered. There is a kind of childlike glee as you feel that particular empowered entity move beyond your Energy-body influence, go out into the dimensions of all our kin, all our relations, to interact more totally as a result of the merging/relationship between you and that entity. If there is anything like compensation involved in what began as an overpowering situation, of healer and healed, teacher and student, guide and seeker, it is that overwhelming feeling of joy as one who, for whatever reason, has lived with a weaker vibration and now moves into the world with a stronger vibration. The reverberations of such an empowering interaction ripple outward wherever, whenever the two involved in the merging interact with other Total Energy-bodies. Total energy growth is cumulative. It may seem very slow in 3D time, but in 4D space-time the expansion may be instantaneous, forever.

Power as we have been speaking of it is often confused with force. We come to the limits of language when trying to describe fourth dimensional realities with three dimensional words. But the distinction between power and force is easily identifiable. Force is not the result of free flowing Total Energy-body transmission. Force is direction set by some form of limitation. Force attempts domination, of another Total Energy-body, of a situation, of some form of emitted energy that is unbound. Force is a distraction which does not empower, but weakens, makes submissive, forms and shapes in terms of a pattern imposed. That pattern will be justified as being rational, as being Law, sometimes divinely given, as being necessary to create stabilization and order in what appears as chaos.

Often in Total Energy-body empowerment situations there is a temptation to maintain what has been created as a result of Total Energy-body Relationship. That urge to hold-on-to, if acted on, moves empowerment to forced non-change. In 3D Newtonian realities we prefer structure and illusions as zones of comfort. We go to a lot of trouble building fences and walls to shore up permanency, on-going-ness. Much of our effort as humans goes into defending patterns, habits, structures of all kinds to keep what appears 'necessary' happening. The whole notion of economy as the basic human interaction is a result of our urge to hold-on-to. When we, for whatever reason, suddenly find ourselves in a Total Energy-body flow situation, it can feel so different, so foreign to our usual habits, that we feel like we are letting-go-of. We feel generative, creative, outpouring energy as an emptying. And many humans react by grabbing tighter, by retreating to all the familiar fences and walls that give them false security. They function in fear. That fear, when projected, generates force and a need to control, which often erupts into confrontation and even violence.

Free-flowing, cosmic energy emissions have sometimes been described as 'the force.' It is interesting to watch story tellers using that terminology. The 'force' is available to characters who use it to dominate other characters. 'The force' can be shaped into weapons. The whole interaction of Total Energy-bodies is twisted into 3D warrior conflict, a message from the dominant culture that distracts as it points at, but does not really enact, 4D reality.

There is a real conflict in 3D reality between those who use any means to dominate, and those who interact freely with all our kin, celebrating cosmic Total Energy-body relationship. This conflict is not new, and may be at least as old as humankind, 40-50 thousand years by some reckonings. For the last five thousand years, domination, rather than Total Energy-body interaction, has propelled generations of humanity forth as conquerors of all beings. Most who live in relation as Total Energy-body beings have suffered the onslaught. Inquisitions of all forms in all cultures have attempted to purge pagan cultures. Genocide has eliminated all but a few who secretly pass on the Total Energy-body interactive process, De-Light. Most of us involved in total energy beingness live outside dominant culture. Many live in remote areas, in the deserts of Australia, Africa, the Southwestern

A Catechism for the Children of De-Light

United States, in the jungles of South America and the far East, in the high mountains of Tibet, the Pyrenees, on the tundra's of the polar regions. Some survive biculturally, living within the dominant culture when necessary, living secret lives of which only others involved in Total Energy-body relationship know. Domination appears to be threatening the very existence of basic, interactive, prolific earth beings, whose continuance is more essential to earth than humans are. The reason for writing this catechism, for passing on Total Energy-body interaction knowledge, is the message that humans must change. If we, and other beings, are to live fully with the earth we need to end our domination and cease our forceful, exploitative ways. We are at a time when human awareness of the need for this change is growing. Yet the effects of dominant-culture-comfort keep us fearful of what such a total change in our beingness would be like. We tend to wish to hold on to what we know. We tend to think of illusions as comforts. We confuse comfort with De-Light.

Some have indicated that printing Total Energy-body knowledge is dangerous, that it should continue to be held in secret. Enactment of Total Energy-body energies happens despite imposed limits. We should interact freely only with those who interact freely, and in the way the universe works, like will be attracted to like, no matter what the forced 3D world condition.

There are times when leadership, guidance and teaching can and should empower humans and all other beings. Humanity is approaching one of these times. If, as children of the cosmos, we can become Total Energy-bodies, feeling the De-Light of creative interaction, we can make different sorts of decisions about how we live our 3D lives. That is why this book is written. It is a tool, laying out essential principles that will help our maturing as an interactive species.

WHAT ABOUT BLACK MAGIC AND TRICKERY?

Power can come through an individual for purposes of healing, leading, giving guidance, and then become twisted and used to gain comfort, prestige, superior position within a community. This black magic process happens quite frequently. Usually, those who succumb to this misuse of free flowing interactive energies are successful in their illusionary actions for a time. Then they lose the power that came through their vessel and act out of desperation. They often pull on power as it comes through others, thieves of a multidimensional nature.

Black magicians can be quite dangerous to the De-Light process. They usually know how energy flows. They also know how it can be disrupted. Often they know how to overpower less intense vibrational fields/bodies. An entity that is engaged in Total Energy-body interaction can sense the presence of a black magician. There is extreme discomfort. Colors are murky, dark. Quite often the field around the black magician feels like potential forced violence.

In a Total Energy-body interaction sometimes one particular Energy-body withdraws, begins setting limits, doesn't function freely. Depending upon the nature of this withdrawal, the tendency for manipulation or forcing the Total Energy-body relationship in a direction has the desperation that leads to black magic interactions.

Black magic interactions are not limited to humans or to human-like entities, such as angels, guides, devas, etc. Total Energy-body relationships between different species, such as humans, fish and trees, can be fully entered into, only to be twisted toward human advantage. Multi-entity decision-making councils have to be very careful to maintain the clarity of all, as energies shift and move. Each entity must continue to feel open, free, able to receive and give totally.

Trickery is another matter. When we are in situations of trying to bring 4D Total Energy-body interactions/sensations into 3D reality/formats, those who are empowered to teach have to use familiar 3D tools, situations, to awaken those of less intense vibration. This is what all ceremony, ritual and storytelling is about. Such tools are not themselves the Total Energy-body interaction.

They are prods, helping humans and others feel that there is more than 3D reality.

If the process of tricking people into sensing, feeling, becoming their potentials, is successful, then those involved will move toward or actually engage in Total Energy-body interactions. If the ceremony, ritual or other form of trickery becomes self-serving, then movement toward limits rather than interactive total energy sharing happens. Sometimes entire institutions are established around certain tricks. Humans become financially dependent upon the existence of these institutions. It can even be taught that Total Energy-body interactions are not possible or are only sanctioned as a result of the existence of these institutions. These institutions are then defended. Wars are fought, because inevitably these institutions clash, claiming territory and souls, claiming that only their form of trickery is proper. We can see these kinds of human interactions of a limited nature everywhere. Perhaps the most dominant continues to be the Church, Mosque, Temple complex.

Trickery is a very delicate process. It is necessary only because we tend not to interact in a Total Energy-body manner. Yet, it is very easy for the trickery, whatever its form, to be substituted for the totally interactive process. There is often power coming through the Trickster. There can also be power twisted into force or even black magic. The Trickster or clown or knowledgeable fool in all cultures embodies all these characteristics. The Trickster as teacher is revered, but her/his position in a culture can easily slip from transmission of total energy interaction knowledge to manipulator.

DOES MEASUREMENT LIMIT TOTAL ENERGY-BODY INTERACTION?

Humans measure. We count things. We recognize patterns. Some of these patterns appear cyclic. For instance, as the relationship of the Sun and the Earth continually changes, soils warm or cool. Basic life forms like bacteria are more active or less active in soils within a rather narrow temperature range. Bacterial activity, along with host of other kinds of interrelationships within warming and cooling soils, governs growth, decay, abundance, scarcity. This is just one of the myriad of great relationship activities that happen whether we as humans are present or not, whether we as humans are aware of that activity or not. Basic, simple, cyclic or rhythmic activities seem more significant than the personal interactions of which we are conscious. Daily interactions between people, between people and animals, or even people and plants, rarely acknowledge the relationships of microorganisms that go on simultaneously. Yet, without those primary microorganism relationships, without the continual interaction of the Sun and the Earth, without literally thousands of life giving interactions that are not necessarily part of our awareness, life would not be. We would not have evolved. Our personhood, at least as it is linked to energy-matter might not be of consequence.

All pagan cultures put a great deal of emphasis on knowledge and awareness of cycles. The ability to predict the rising and setting cycle of the Sun at a given location is important if you are reliant on farming for sustenance. The long-term observations and precise calculations by the astronomer-mathematicians of the Maya, noting for example that the Morningstar, the Full Moon, and the Sun all make life-giving appearances at the same time, though rarely, but on a cycle that can be calculated, meant to them that the universe is ordered, that earthquakes and other cataclysmic events are not the normal state of energy-matter affairs. The cultures of India in 5,000 BCE delineated a cosmic energy pattern which they described in terms of eight signs that had characteristics very much like the characteristics of familiar animals that seemed to appear as star patterns (constellations) in the night sky. The detailed observations of the night sky behind this cosmology was, given the necessity for keen observance when survival was dependent upon hunting or being hunted, not magical, or even unusual. Humans took that pattern west to the Fertile Crescent, and the Astrologers of Babylonian culture, which survived desert conditions, determined that the pattern of eight was really a pattern of twelve signs of the zodiac. According to their cosmology, birth during a certain sign gave an individual certain tendencies toward being in the material-energy relationship web in predictable ways. All these cultures in their cosmologies, and the observations behind them, reveal human beings as calculators, counters, measurers, and in very complex fashion. The cycles are everywhere, cycles that are greater than any single event-relationship, greater than any personal action. They are often reflections of patterns that are themselves very complex energy-matter interactions, such as the Chinese zodiac, made up of animals arranged in the order as they appeared to Buddha, but reflecting the energy of solar years in a cycle of twelve.

It is necessary to fully appreciate all cyclic patterns, for they are the pinnacle of the human capacity to recognize, to calculate, to see order and beauty in what otherwise might be understood as a chaotic, even frightening universe. Yet, do these patterns actually exist? Or are they human projections?

If innumerable energy-matter relationships exist in recognizable cyclic or pattern form, does that mean that we humans, we individuals are merely parts within that pattern? Are our lives determined? Are we predestined to live out certain actions, interact in terms of mathematically predictable tendencies? Is there free will?

Pagan cultures teach Total Energy-body interrelationship. Total! As a Total Energy-body person we are creatures of the Sun, of microorganisms in the soil, of plankton in the oceans, of grasses and trees and all plant life, of all animals, all gases, all minerals, all unseen energies, of planets interacting at a given time in our solar system, of galaxies whirling, of universes expanding. We are Total Energy Beings. In any given moment we interact within all that totalness. We *do* choose. But when we choose, we choose within all kinds of wave energies and manifestations into matter-energy that infuse our choosing. The more our choices are made in the light of awareness of cosmic complexity, the more we are using our attention and intention to choose in terms of our place within larger relationships, then the easier it is for us to live in daily energy-matter, earth reality. Our problems as humans are usually traceable to making choices that are not within the scope of greater cycles and patterns of which we are a part.

So the question comes, how do we stay attuned to our greater realities? In pagan cultures the most revered people are the Wise Ones. They are those who have not only lived long, they are those who for whatever reason are most continuously attuned to the greater flow. They are astrologers, shamans, knowledgeable fools, trickster teachers, story tellers. While the culture itself teaches and nurtures greater cosmic awareness, as a moment-to-moment necessity, the Wise Ones are sought out to help with focus, able to train our resistors so we are able to handle more and more Total Energy. In our day, books often act as a substitute for teachings. But books can only skim the surface of an individual's potential. Interaction with a Wise One has presence and impact of a different order. We can learn of cycles and patterns from books, but that learning can lead to entrapment if we do not learn that Total Energy-body alertness requires being part of those cycles, requires total interaction with all the forces of continual creation, requires the capacity to feel De-Light.

Considerations in decision-making based on Part X

1. Real decisions must include our relations.
2. Total Energy-bodies recognize each other.
3. Councils of Total Energy-bodies, if diverse, can make informed decisions about how to live *with* Earth.
4. Real power promotes life.
5. Trickery, while necessary, can be misused.
6. Cycles and patterns disclose grander orderings for our acknowledgment and celebration.

PART XI
PRINCIPLES OF
ENVISIONING A FUTURE

A Catechism for the Children of De-Light

WHAT IS MOST IMPORTANT FOR CONSIDERATION?

We raise questions of principle to help us with human decision-making. When we speak based upon vision, we see broadly. We are as the eagle, high above, looking at the earthly condition as a whole. There are not many eagles, when you compare them with the numbers of rodents and microorganisms. Consideration of dimensional realities is not usually discussed around board room tables as 3D reality is manipulated. Yet, without broad perceiving we grow more and more limited as a thinking/managerial species. We are more rigid, risking our very existence because we are short-sighted, linear, fear-filled.

We start, with this Catechism, to raise questions about the nature of all of reality and all dimensions—here on this planet and beyond. We should be aware of that of which we are a part, aware of where we come from, aware of the Cosmic Mother whose vastness is barely imaginable, as we look to her for birth. Our particular birth here is within just one of millions of galaxies— whirling, constantly moving, continually creating—the centers and design of De-Light. We should continually be cognizant of how the Sun, which is the center of our being, our earthly manifestation, feeds all life on this planet, allows for creative out-pouring in reflection of its own continual light-giving. We should continually be thankful and grateful for other forms of life on this water planet, for simple bacteria, for plankton, for grasses, for trees and vegetation of all kinds. Without the interaction of these 'beings' with the Sun and Moon and all other beings, humans would cease to be. We should bring all of these creative-being relationships into each of our decisions, for we humans are never alone. When we decide to build any artifact we should do so in agreement with all other life, enhancing that life, bringing forth solar/galactic glory and generating De-Light.

It may seem impractical to make decisions with such an overview and the considerations it illuminates, but if we make decisions that do not reflect the whole, as it is continually chang-ing, then we are erecting edifices with no galactic purpose. Even an ant hill community fulfills a purpose by tilling soil and recycling decaying wood. So we humans, with our unique electromagnetic body/brain capacity should make decisions utilizing all our capabilities for Total Energy-body galactic reflection.

WHAT MIGHT A FULLY RESONATE WORLD FEEL/LOOK LIKE?

Humans build and rebuild our 3D realities. Our daily   lives are made up of time schedules oriented to institutions. We sleep in our various shelters, go from these shelters for work, play, education, worship and return to our shelters for food and human sharing. Our bodily lodges and the houses and apartments that shield us from the elements are usually understood as our base, our home. We usually make decisions in terms of what keeps our personal routine in relation to our daily schedule/home base. Especially in urban conditions, where most of us live, decisions involving larger considerations of life dimensions are rare. When we are not living the 'rat race' we are watching it, being entertained with stories that are of how others are running the same narrowly defined race(s), sometimes in the forms of sports.

What if you are a sensitive human being who continually feels the galactic hum, who senses De-Light? How do you 'be' a Total Energy-body, interacting in constant creation?

First of all, it is extremely important to remember/feel, that you are never alone. You will feel lonely, like an alien, when confronted with the noisy maze of the traffic of everyday life. But be aware that there are many other sensitized humans like yourself. The trick is how we might recognize each other. There are, even in the deepest urban canyons, birds, trees and a few plants, even grasses pushing up through the pavement, living there as reminders. There are our ancestors, those who have gone before us, some of whom love earth and are here in non-material dimensions as teachers, guides, companions. There are microorganisms, active and breathing Energy-bodies, even in the cement of cities.

A Catechism for the Children of De-Light

Vibrant life is everywhere around us. It may seem easier to be attuned to life energies in the forests or prairies or on a farm, but cities also are full of life potential.

How do we recognize another Total Energy-body resonance? Sometimes we give each other visible signs. We wear necklaces or earrings or other jewelry or clothing that signal our conscious awareness through culturally accepted, agreements about the meaning(s) of costume. More often eyes are a clue.

Eyes reflect the galactic/solar whirl. Eyes are amazing watery pools, filled with design and color. Eyes are where energy is most easily seen/sensed. Total Energy-body emanations are like fire. When that fire comes forth from within a sensitive person it is visible and palpable. There is a brightness, a vibrancy from within the eyes. As a De-light-filled sensitive person, you feel another like yourself. You feel the "I am you are me." This feeling is only a clue, but it is a gift of recognition on which you can act. We often say we have intuitive insight about another human. You do. As you learn to trust your insights by checking them out, you begin to move more freely as a Total Energy-body.

Human beings have the potential of expressing De-Light through emanations projected and received through our solar plexus, that area of energy beneath the navel which is a whirling, energy transmitting center, reflective of whirlwinds on the planet and galaxies like our Milky Way. Human transmissions of solar-paramagnetic energy link us with all beings. We all transmit wave energies. But those humans who are aware of such transmissions, who direct them, who send them with intention, create unique energy sensations that affect those around them. Often sensitive solar beings, their emanations of energy bathing others like a fresh breeze next to a waterfall, attract those who are less sensitive and feel energized by this contact. Consciously aware solarized beings, by their very presence, like a sun, raise the consciousness of others who are less aware or unaware. Or, when we meet another like ourselves, we immediately feel attunement, alignment, agreement. We *know* each other in the most total sense of knowing. There is no need to explore, to guess, for we are instantly as one, even though we are individually, unique collections of experience. "I am you are me" is felt intensely. There are no barriers; all is possible.

What if the majority of human beings interacted in this way, totally, daily, all over the planet? What if we realized our Total Energy-body potentials? Our priorities would change. If it was a primary directive in all decision-making to agree to create Total Energy interactions, then life would be oriented around celebration rather than economic measurements of successful 3D material manipulations. Let us look at an example. The local food co-op store is making decisions about expansion. After 25 years and many expansions, once again success seems to dictate either building another store or adding on to the current store. The kinds of considerations raised by staff and community members are typically: charts of economic data, comparisons with other stores in other locations, fears that another store will come in and take market share, and unpleasant crowding of the store's narrow aisles when rat race time schedules force people to shop in off business hours, etc. Now, what if we look at the organism of the community store as a Total Energy-body? What is its purpose? How might it function? Currently most of what is on the shelves in this store is brought into this locality from some distance, by truck. Like most humans, the energy flow is one of taking in, bringing from outside. Then, obviously, the purpose of the store is deliverance, distribution of these outside goods. Very little comes from this store as a result of generation by members. The store is not really grounded in local production energy. It is vulnerable as a economic entity dependent upon volatile forces such as the availability of fossil fuel. If this store were the deliverance channel for local farmer/growers, craftspeople, if it were truly a market where the collective energy of a locality was reflected, it would be a very different place. For one thing, total community need for stimulation of total energy capacity realization would have everyone in the locale somehow connected to the cooperative process of, in this case, making the highest quality human diet available to all, in cooperation with all other species. That decision to make that diet available would be based on agreement about what is needed to stimulate Total Energy-body interaction, which is the grander purpose for having a food delivery focal point, or store. Decisions about how to run a cooperative store showcase all the limitations of a 3D reality that is not solarized. Along with crucial considerations of diet related to the overall purpose of Total Energy-body interactions of all beings, simple considerations of solarized refrigeration, heat, water delivery should all be on the table. In fact, once we recognize what is *needed* to live as highly resonant Energy-bodies in kinship with all other beings, it becomes clear that we must retool all our shelters and delivery systems to reflect our true purpose. The greater life unity as purpose for conscious humans on this planet requires that we act, individually and collectively, as though we recognize our roles as transmitters of cosmic life giving energy. There is a delicateness in our actions once we fully remember what it is like to be a Total Energy-body freely interacting. If you have experienced the tenderness of lovers, the feeling is similar, but with all beings, all the time.

In a fully resonate world we no longer see ourselves or understand ourselves as pagan, a distinctly derogatory term labeling our consciousness negatively. Rather we walk with the sun and the other stars. We know that we are solarized beings, galactic transmitters of all the forces of creation, moment to moment, always. We stand tall and our eyes sparkle with that awareness. We live as teachers of continual change, each being a whirlwind reflecting the galactic whirl. We know our androgyny and recognize both the female and male aspects of all others as we reflect the Cosmic Mother/Father.

Resonance with Earth is celebrated by us, daily. In our prayers and in our actions we feel the living soils. We sense the millions of microorganisms, arthropods, nematodes and others that inhabit just one handful of rich living soil. We give thanks for their being, for all their Total Energy-body interactions, for without their activity, stimulated and fed by the sun, we would not have life. Humans should be doing everything we can do to feed, to give energy to help build this planet's soils so that the rich fertility of a garden can be everywhere, in hopes that desertification is reversed as human legacy. In a world of total resonance, positive earth building should be a human activity replacing war. If we trained ourselves, spent the time and effort and money for soil building that we spend on keeping war machines going, we could bring about a whole new soil-earth, working cooperatively with millions of other species. Once we focus on creating healthy garden-like soils, then trees and all other plant life can thrive amongst us. And even more critically, once plant life is regenerated, the magic of atmospheric water interaction with earth can again function fully, seasonally, for drought is a condition reflecting human mismanagement, greed, destructive activity.

In a totally resonate world Water is sacred. The free movement of great rivers and streams is part of the resonate song. Damming must only be done, if at all, in such a way as to not stop stream flow and fish movement, as well as the rush of air in water and around water as it moves toward the seas. Diversions should build in the type of flow patterns that mimic natural water ways, that energize and purify their currents. Sacred water used by humans should be designed so that many uses are made of it before it returns to the earth or the sea. Dwellings need to be plumbed so that recirculated water is used for all secondary needs, such as cooling, gardening and washing where fresh water is not actually needed.

Air—the atmosphere—is treated with total reverence in a fully resonate world. As we interact in a total energy way, we continually create situations which stimulate ion balances. Air, like soil, is alive. We must do all that we can do as humans to eliminate our waste from air. For that waste is a sign of our irreverence. It is a sign of our non-recognition of our solar-beingness. Air cannot be allowed to be a fossil fuel dump. In a totally resonate world air would be protected, realizing that all living beings need the best atmosphere this planet can offer if we are to reflect the creative urges of the Cosmic Mother/Father.

Resonance, Total Energy-body interactions, is like fire. It is like the fire of all the suns of all the galaxies. It is the continual creation of the two-becoming-one. It is De-Light; Fire-light drives, energizes, all that every being does. Fire-light is within each being from the smallest microbe to the sun itself, propelling all that we are capable of being. Fire creates as it consumes. Fire is supremely transformative, a continual reminder that all is change, all is motion. No human conception, not even our broadest attempts at understanding, reflected in the principles in this Catechism, are permanent, unchanging, everlasting. Many solar based cultures (perceived as pagan by the dominant culture) constructed stone edifices into which they designed cosmic understanding, measurement, reverence. Some of these structures have endured thousands of solar seasons. But in the geologic scope of planetary history, even these masterpieces of human achievement become just compost, new life. What continues is motion, creation, continual generation from explosions of two-becoming-one, moving out into relationship with other creations, other resonance, on and on, beyond any of our conceptions of space or time.

Much of what limits our Total Energy-body interactions is a result of human *want* rather than *need*. Want is engendered by culture. We want new cars, all kinds of distractive entertainments, big houses full of electronic convinces, gourmet restaurant foods, etc. What humans need is another matter. Need must be assessed within the flow of all wave energies. For instance, if we continue to fill electromagnetic wave energy fields with television, radio and phone transmissions we are catering to high speed human convenience. What are we doing to other beings, whose sensitivity to that same energy, makes them suffer from human generated background interference noise? What are we doing to humans, who are continually affected by electromagnetic disturbance? At a cellular level all beings, linked by DNA life chains on Earth, are pulsing at about 8 megahertz. When that pulse is overpowered, electronically by humans, cells are weakened. Cellular orientation can be changed by very subtle paramagnetic manipulation. All bodily functions are at risk, especially those that are nerve dependent, like the brain. Still, we continue to want conveniences based on microwave activity. We want a lot of other human oriented processes and 'stuff,' much of which limits our abilities to totally interact with each other and with all other life.

What do we need? Foods to continue the bio-chemical-physical bodies continual growth. These foods need to be grown and harvested and prepared with continual cognizance of Kin. The fruit is the seed, the seed is the fruit. All that we take into our beings becomes us, becomes our health or our sickness. We have the knowledge as a technologically aware culture to design diets that feed our abilities to interact as Total Energy-bodies. These diets usually look quite different from diets that feed conflict and violence, warfare and bloodshed. If we were to turn our sciences toward human need as a reflection of the total energy flow of all relationships on earth and throughout the galaxy, turn away from conquering as a goal which expresses want rather than need, then our primary daily activity would change significantly.

Humans need shelter. We are not covered with thick coats like Bison. Even in tropical climates, we need to seek refuge from rain and wind. Some shelters have been and can be very simple, made with locally available vegetation and clay. Some need to be thick-walled, to be sturdy enough to withstand snow loads. In modern times, buildings have been constructed with access to cheap fossil fuel, allowing for heated or cooled interiors. We do not need climates balanced in this way. We have gotten used to them and want them. What if all shelters were retooled with a solar orientation? What if all our design energies moved us past the era of fossil fuel dependency and into a truly solarized world? Some of these technologies are in place, in isolated urban, suburban and rural areas. But as a species, we have not committed to solarizing. Shelters would look and feel quite differently if our Sun were their focus. Light and heat would not be pollutive in a truly solarized future. Structures would be stone, glass or clay. Earth lodges, even individual homes, need to reflect our collective understanding of our place and role in the ever creative generation of galactic life. All proportions, placement, orientation should be the result of reflective measurements, as were the pyramids of Egypt and Central America and possibly Mars. Human consciousness of our kinship with all beings and processes of creation should be built into structures that will last for centuries. Shelter is one of our primary human means of teaching each other through sign and symbol. All our shelters should be placed with garden quality vegetation as a primary consideration. Significant amounts of foods can be produced utilizing solar principles and designing buildings to include spaces in which heat seeking vegetation can thrive. Solarized urban and suburban living situations could be very productive and beautiful, giving residents nourishment, beauty, and purpose.

Another form of shelter is clothing. Clothing does and should reflect who we are. If we realize our Total Energy-body potentials, clothing should reflect that understanding. Bright robes and ceremonial type dress often project solar-galactic understanding among pagan peoples. Adorning ourselves with feathers and animal hides, and other remnants of life from our Kin on this planet, show our respect and honor for these other distinct ways of being and perceiving, as we move about in daily life, reflecting their lives. Much of the intent of daily ceremonial clothing has been set aside by the distractions of the current dominant culture. Clothing should have purpose that reflects our intent to enter Total Energy-body interactions, moment to moment, in our lives.

Like buildings which reflect solar purpose and intent, clothing should be made of plant and animal life that is sturdy and renewable. Linen, silk, hemp and other fibers should replace synthetic fabrics which are fossil fuel dependent and made to wear out. Fads created by designers who represent dominant corporate profit makers, should be replaced by designer-teachers—highly trained solarized beings whose clothing is made to last, whose clothing language is a daily statement expressing who we are and what we are.

A joyous sense of belonging, as we realize our solar-galactic purpose, is very important. This sense of belonging to the process of life's unfolding needs to be a daily celebration everywhere. Every human task should be part of that celebration: All food preparation, from growing to serving meals; all lodge building, from construction of buildings to teaching the young of their sacred earth lodges, their Total Energy-bodies and how they are related to all other beings; all transference of knowledge through any human language, art, writing, music, dance, attuned to galactic De-Light; all news about how the process of life unfolds for humans on this planet, not how materiality was again thwarted, derailed, mismanaged by the dominant culture; all interactions being Total Energy-body potentials unfolding. This symphony of human joy interacting with all other beings could bring this planet to its galactic potential; fullness, ripeness, continual renewal; a solarized jewel sparkling in the universal womb of the Cosmic Mother.

We can do this. We need to choose to do this, to shift our basic agreements. We need to make consistent decisions to live solarized lives.

HOW CAN HUMANS LEARN TO LIVE MULTIDIMENSIONAL LIVES FILLED WITH DE-LIGHT?

What do most people reading this book touch, feel, see, hear, sense in daily life? Take time to make a list of your typical daily activities. Look at this list from the point of view of Total Energy-body interaction. Notice areas of continual creative expression, of De-Light coming through, opportunities for agreement with all beings, for bringing forth earth potential. Notice limitation, fear, defensive posturing.

Most urban-suburban dwellers are caught in a routine of habits that find direct support within the dominant culture. Our speedy daily lives distract us from multidimensional fulfillment by offering immediate gratification supported by manufactured convenience. We need to break our habits, our addictions. Taking several hours a day to participate in life-enhancing activities—to meditate, practice yoga, garden, be with natural processes in some very basic interactive way, like collecting seeds, making love, doing a ceremony to celebrate the changes of the moon—would help us shift our lives. We need to gain direction for our individual being so that it can freely and consciously interact with all other beings, with full attention and intention.

How we do this is simple. Each of us is capable of being all that we are capable of becoming: a reflection of the total galactic cosmos. We are the stars. We are planets. We are all the water and vegetation and animals and insects and microorganisms of planet earth. And we are all the potential electromagnetic, paramagnetic forces that make the unity of life much more than is accounted for by the dominant human culture in the industrial-technological era. So, start taking time to step away from distraction. Just do it, cold turkey. Stop giving energy to people and processes which limit your capability for full interaction. Start giving energy, time, attention and intention to what is life-giving. Sometimes human relationships are where this process can begin, two people becoming one in direction, finding creation in the Total Energy-body lifestream. Sometimes human interaction can be a major distraction. Your galactic sense of unfoldment and purpose might best be nurtured by gardening, alone, with all of nature surrounding you. The possible pursuits, to enhance our connection to our lives, surround us: meditation, prayer and preparation for ritual celebrations; planting trees of every kind, everywhere; creating water flows and streams, filled with aquatic life; walking around a city finding its potential nature—buildings as canyons, people as all the reflections of animals, reptiles, birds or insects.

Finding reflections and companionship with other human beings to share this process of transformation, this change in daily activity to be in agreement with all life, may seem initially to be rare, but right here in the heart of the materialistic sprawl there are millions of us. Together we must share our feelings, insights and perspectives. And very importantly, as Children of De-Light we must keep alive the De-Light that comes with conception and birth on this planet, that is in young children's eyes and fantasies and hopes, before the dominant culture thwarts, limits, diverts attention from basic attunement to sensing Total Energy-body currents. We must become active transmitters, encouraging, coaxing, nudging each other with stories, music, dance, and life-giving activity. In short, we must become a human culture with a planetary-inter planetary, total energy consciousness. We must become our potential right now, not in some far off future, or in Heaven or some other afterlife.

All of this unfolding is a matter of moment to moment decision-making. Our choices create our lives. If we allow other people, with agendas of manipulation and greed, to control us, that is a concession we make. If we choose to live in galactic harmony with all beings, then we must act that way, not just think and talk that way. Such actions will bring about drastic changes in how the collective human community interacts. It will mean agree-ments that are immediate, directions that will change everything from food, to shelter, to clothing, to how we spend our time each day. Much of our 'entertainment' for example, is irrelevant to galactic unfoldment as human/all being purpose. If we stop giving energy to that industry and create in its place ceremony and ritual which utilizes some of the technology of that industry, while promoting Total Energy-body interactions, incredible change would result. If we changed our view of political-economic reality to one based on intraspecies energy interactions, almost all our notions of "resource usage" and "investment" would fall away. In their place balanced species interactions would have humans as part of the mix, but not the management part, not the profit at the expense of others part.

Listen to the 'news,' its focus, its beat. When it is not report-ing on bloodshed, it is reporting on great financial victories, which are always at the expense of other species. The news reports the successes and failures of the dominant culture's conquering, its attempts to control nature. It is not news at all. It is 'olds,' the same old story dressed up with filler for the particular day. 'News' would be that humans decided to live in harmony, to build and eat in harmony. How we do that might for a while be exciting news, only because the contrast would be so different, and we are attuned to news and entertainment as an expression of dualism. But, once we begin acting in consistent consort with Total Energy-body expressions, teaching stories of unfoldment(s) would stimulate others toward risking creativity each and every moment of our lives, in agreements with all others toward rising creativity and in agreements with all other life forms. Alert living does not allow for us to be observers. We never are truly observers either as scientists or as television watchers. We are dimensionally involved, whether we acknowledge involvement or not. We are Total Energy-bodies, whether or not we recognize how all life interaction works. Without recognition we fool ourselves into thinking that somehow we are outside process, that we are as Gods, able to manipulate, control, direct, manage, when in reality we are reflections of all that we consider somehow different from ourselves.

The key to being a freely interacting Total Energy-body is to assess the agreements you currently use for daily decision-making. Do you agree with the dominant culture that money is power? Do you base your daily routine on the seeming need for cash flow? Most of us do. So what if you shift that basic agreement? What if you recognize money, and the need to obtain money, as entrapment? Does that mean that you quit your job? No! Not necessarily. It may mean that you go to your 'job' (whatever it is) with a wholly different attitude. Say you work in manufacturing. Perhaps the hands-on tooling of a piece of plastic or metal allows you to meet with other people during breaks or lunch to plan how that manufacturing machinery could be used for the retooling, the solarization of human life support systems. Opportunities are everywhere for beginning the changes. Most important for you are your agreements as they are expressed as attention and energy involvement. If you give your Total Energy to a process direction, make sure it is one that is in agreement with how you see/understand the greater reality. Otherwise you will feel torn.

During this time of transformation many of us who are sensitives, trying to allow total energy expressions, feel a kind of cultural half-breed condition. We find ourselves living lives split between two very different realities. On the one hand we came into a materialistically driven reality that is fundamentally dualistic in nature. We learned from parents, teachers, ministers, priests or rabbis, how to live morally dualistic lives. As we mature and learn/sense the greater universal galactic realities of which we are but one species, we begin to see the destructive nature of that dualism, even in its highest moral forms. We sense anthropomorphism—human centeredness—everywhere, and we struggle to get beyond its limitations. We make new agreements with all other life. We begin to act and think differently. It is very difficult to find daily balance as a cultural half-breed. Living within paradox can be supremely creative, or it can feel stifling, overwhelming, since the feeling of Total Energy-body flow is so much different from what most people have experienced.

HOW DO WE ACHIEVE BALANCE WHILE LIVING WITH PARADOX?

If you seek the peace that comes from being attuned with all other life, set aside a period each and every day to sense the totality of Total Energy-body interaction.

Usually, this means removing yourself from the destructive interferences of the dominant, materially oriented, culture. Remove yourself from telephones, television, computers, cars, radios, and where possible, from the subtle influences of electrical lines running through walls, air conditioning systems, stimulants like caffeine and alcohol, diets that generate highs and lows. I find the best time to do this is very early in the morning, just before dawn. In India and much of the far East, and among many native American sensitives, this time, known as the hour of the wolf, is utilized for prayer and mediation. It is best to be outside among the elements, but that is not necessary. You need to sit or stand in agreement with the outpouring of life energy of all life. There are many formal practices passed on by solarized cultures that aid in attunement with all possible energy transmissions. Many sit cross-legged, hands laid open, palms up, eyes closed and focused on the center of the forehead between the eyes. Breath is in some practices a matter of ritual patterns used to achieve various energy balances. In deep meditation where breath is not part of the focus, breathing is often very slow At this time of day your awareness is on the fact that you are everything. You are all wave energies, all creations. Your Total Energy-body is in a receptive mode being prepared for a day in which you will of necessity be in a mode of transmission, of giving, or creative going-forth. You are as a sacred structure, a temple or a cathedral or a mosque, not as a shell, but as a potentially radiant moving symbol within all of creation and especially human communities.

All galactic-solarized cultures (considered pagan by the dominant culture) suggest that the initiate focus on cosmic light, its source(s), while in the meditative agreement mode. You are being filled during this time. When you feel filled, at One, in cosmic agreement with all life and life giving creative process, you are ready to interact with the materially oriented world where, unfortunately, most people at this time are not sharing this agreement. You are charged, as it were, like a battery, with cosmic energy that will carry you through a day. In conditions where stresses are severe, you may need another charging session later in the day, although the background interference noise of the material world makes it more difficult to feel free energy as the dynamos whirl. As cosmic light fills your Total Energy Being you will feel/sense your brightness. For another looking at you from the outside, you will glow with intensity, like a candle that has been lit.

What to do with all that energy? Do not throw it away. Transmit it carefully, in a healing manner. Whatever you do during the day will reflect the quiet reverence you carry. Your creative self will be a source of light for many others. Some may try to crush that light. Some may try to steal it. Give, but be aware of how you are giving, where the energy that comes through you is going. Be aware of your interactions as relationships, and know that all energy relationships yield birth, as well as all kinds of potential life.

WHAT IS LEADERSHIP

Decision-making, as a function of how humans are to interact with all other life, often occurs without consideration of the principles written here. The mass culture generally makes decisions based on hopes of financial reward.

A real question for galactic sensitives is whether or not we need to participate in the decision-making apparatus of the dominant culture. If we are to participate, how much energy and time should we give to raising solarized voices? Isn't this point of view so foreign to most people that to bring it forth as a political reality is a waste, throwing pearls before swine, as it were?

If humans are here to learn the effects of limitation in the material dimensions, once we know even some of how all beings actually interrelate at cellular, energy wave levels, then we have a responsibility to share what we have learned. Each sensitive's insight is a valued contribution to the collective human understanding of Kinship with all life. Storytelling and teaching keep alive solar cultural understandings. There are many mechanisms for doing this, from school room participation, to making books and movies, to presenting skits or pageants or plays at ritual times of the year.

The decision to promote change toward Total Energy-body awareness, galactic interactions of all life, solarized retooling of material reality, sets up real alternative stories. Utilizing the principles set forth in this catechism we can make the decision to envision and bring about as great a dimensional unfolding as possible within the limitations of the material world. We see and feel potential for whole new interactive directions that would glorify the highest qualities of all beings rather than giving in to mediocrity or even base or crass qualities. As leaders, we decide to create a world where all creatures feel De-Light, all the time. Some may dismiss our leadership as utopian fantasy. But all the creatures of earth are at a major crisis point because of human error. The situation according to the brightest of the dominant culture's scientists is critical. If we sit by and do not step forth at this time, the vision needed for change will not be in decision-making circles.

Do we attempt to bring galactic solarization, Total Energy-body interrelationship of all Kin, as a program based on vision into the mainstream? Do we put together a political agenda to run against the dominant culture? At a 3D level, yes. But we must begin to think about all our interactions dimensionally. The dominant materialistic-corporate culture has set the rules for their kind of world. To fall into playing by those rules would debase all our understanding. The most effective way for our vision to materialize is to make it happen ourselves. How each of us relates with another human, as well as all other species, how we feel the powerful energies of continual creation move through us daily, moment to moment, how all of our interactions reflect our sensibilities, that will make a difference, to us and to others. There are others like ourselves, everywhere. If we recognize each other and interact creatively, supporting each other, we can live differently. We live in dimensional flow with the seasonal outpouring of the trees, grasses, all vegetation. We live with streams and rocks and all the animals, birds, reptiles and insects. We feel continually the humming energy interactions of billions of microorganisms per square foot of soil . We live with awareness of ionization changes in the air we all share. Most importantly, we try to live our human lives in such a way that our impact on other lives is minimal. This is not a negative purpose. It is an attempt to raise human potential to creative heights of fulfillment that give us multidimensional, galactic purpose. As a thinking species we set about to demand more than survival. We want the best for ourselves and all our Kin.

Leadership in this sense will be creating a way of being and becoming which lives beside the dominant culture. We are not about creating a counterculture. That is a dualistic trap which the dominant culture controls. We simply live a different way with entirely different sets of choices. There will be those in our solarized culture who will emerge as leaders. These will be people of vision and dedicated purpose. Often, these leaders may emerge from what the dominant culture refers to as indigenous peoples. Some cultures have maintained stories and teachings throughout generations beside and outside the genocidal practices of the dominant culture. There are scattered bands of indigenous peoples who are keepers, of Time, of Direction, of Purpose. There are a few indigenous people who have also taken up an education in the ways of the dominant culture. These are cultural half-breeds, and they share a split vision with many of us who were born into the dominant culture and learned to share vision as the result of teaching and ritual interactions with indigenous native peoples. What we must do together is create a worldwide galactic culture, which will find resonance with all peoples and all beings. If we do this together we will attract others. Our living patterns will incorporate more and more total energy harmonies. The resonance of solarized beings caring for each other and caring for every moment grows from the center outward. The more we show others by example how humans can live simply, lightly, happily with the planet, the greater will be everyone's De-Light in living.

WHAT ABOUT THOSE WHO WOULD CONTROL FOR THEIR OWN GLORY AND GAIN?

Throughout human history men, and a few notorious women, have murdered and maimed creation. Trapped in the limitations of their egos and its fear, anger, jealousy and greed, their sickness sets the course for millions of humans who follow their example. In fact, the whole sacredness of history in Western cultures is a testament to warfare, not De-Light. How is it that these planetary criminals get to control destiny? Are humans really that stupid? Many answer yes, and acquiesce to what seems so large a monster that it appears impossible to get out of its grasp. Modern corporate culture is the current manifestation of this warfare consciousness. At every juncture in public discourse, corporate culture plays on fear, anger, jealousy, gaining a stranglehold on collective human consciousness.

Should we confront these gross beings? No! For two reasons. The first is that they are in fact murderers. They use both governmental and private sources to kill any and all beings who are in their *way*. So, stay out of their way! That means that we cleverly appear to play along with them. The second reason not to be trapped in confrontation with corporate culture is that even giving negative energy or confrontive energy to their purposes gives that sickness lethal advantage. Since attention focuses energy we can inadvertently support our adversaries by confrontation. To collectively envision a future without the overwhelming influence of modern mass culture we need to think of how we go about re-tooling, re-symbolizing, re-nurturing, and then set about doing it. There may be times when certain parts of a whole new human infrastructure become vulnerable to conquerors or corporate murderers. Their bursts of violence are alive only as long as they use military style weaponry, for people's commitments have already begun to shift away from rule with guns and greed centered lies about reality. All the collective beings of the planet, and their life force, are stronger than any temporary militant control. Why? Because if you are feeling the fullness of kinship with all life, dimensionally, it is this very beingness itself that fulfills, gives that strength of light which cannot be conquered, burned or murdered by the dominant militarily structured culture. They are severely limited by the very action of continued reliance on the manufacture of armaments and implied agreements that death is to be feared. Without fear they can not rule.

A Catechism for the Children of De-Light

IS THE INDUSTRIAL TECHNOLOGICAL AGE THE HIGH POINT OF HUMANNESS?

The dominant culture would have us believe that industrial technology is the crown of all of creation. In a dimensional assessment of planetary well-being, just the opposite would appear to be the case. If we compare the industrial city with its millions of people to cliff dwellings with hundreds of people in an earlier era, we see that simple technologies are really all that is needed to sustain life. The civilizing force works to create more complicated 'needs.' Those needs are not basic, and are therefore maintained only through addiction. Dominant culture is much like a euphoric drug. The continual high seems wonderful, comfortable, making life almost effortless, while actually being destructive to the drugged person and all that surrounds him or her.

As with all addicted people, any suggestion that priorities should be shifted away from 'high' comfort zones is greeted with defensiveness and violent displays of possessive behavior. In the case of the dominant culture, the human high is supported by the dominant culture religions. The God(s) choose and inaugurate their representatives who bless and invest in industrial technology, its inherent hierarchies reflecting those of the Church, Mosque or Temple.

Looking from a multidimensional viewpoint at the masses of humans clustered in industrial cities at this time, two vibrations are most obvious, plastic and fear. Plastics are how easy access to nonrenewable oil has allowed corporate culture Gods into every life. Look around you. Where I sit, much of what I rely on daily from communication, convenience, doing all that I do, is cheap enough to afford because of plastic. Steel too plays such a role but the dominant culture really 'benefits' the majority of people, giving them the comfort of the high, from plastic. Plastic radios and televisions set the tone of our days. Plastic phones keep us in touch, allow us to reach beyond isolation. Plastics allow computers to be manufactured for every desk, giving users a feeling that they are empowered. The addictive tools are everywhere.

A Catechism for the Children of De-Light

The real question is, do these tools heighten our awareness of our totality, of our relatedness with all other beings? Or do they continue to sweep us up in the illusion of superiority?

Compare the sensitivity of the hunter-gatherer human to today's industrial-technological human. What does survival mean for each? Do both require alertness to all other life, moment to moment, for survival? The hunter-gatherer-farmer lives with paradox each second, knowing and acting as if life/death, hope/fear, fullness/starvation are of his/her making and not outside the human grasp. As a member of the galactic/solar dimensions of all life, the hunter-gatherer-farmer lives awake, aware, being in touch with immediacy of each moment. Her/his senses are dimensional. All beingness, including invisible beings, is part of the energy transmissions moving through his/her body. As an attuned instrument he/she seeks harmony with all other instruments. Harmony, not control for comfort. Industrial technology may be the manifestation of a low degree of humanness. To be our total potential as Energy-body transmitters we have to be able to step aside from its collective impact on every moment of our days.

The technologies themselves are addictive, but are they wrong? Shouldn't the human brain be able to manifest conception into the material plane without disruption to other beings, without threatening survival? Humans are builders. We do have needs for food, clothing, and shelter. These needs could be met for everyone in ways that would be far less destructive of other species. For instance, we have the technologies and could develop others to build and rebuild all our buildings so as to be solar efficient, requiring very small amounts of fossil fuel backup. We could use solar power to charge batteries for transportation. We could stop the throw-away-consciousness, build to last, retool everything so that rather than profit, durability would be the goal. Of course this very suggestion threatens a worldwide market economy where fad through advertising rules, where people change cars like they change clothes, where whatever is new is thought to be better.

A Catechism for the Children of De-Light

Higher pay and job security are the focus for people hooked on progress through technology, so that they can participate fully in purchase power. Set aside that rat race and what have you got? The fear of the unknown. So total is the shift from two and three dimensional focus to four and multidimensional focus that when you are hooked on the dominant culture's prescription for happiness (house, two cars, two children, good job, nice church, good shopping), it is totally scary to even think that there may be another, much more life-giving way of being, of feeling our humanness in Total Energy-body interrelatedness.

HOW COULD WE LIVE WITHOUT THE FOCUS OF 'STUFF'?

Seeing the world as though humans were the reason for existence, limits our creative abilities. The humanistic fallacy keeps us trapped. Once we see ourselves as resonant transmitters, galactic-solar energies whose purpose is to live in interrelationship with all other beings consciously every moment, then how we do this, what is needed to support this, becomes clear. We come in, are born, each of us, with this very delicate mission. To be that purpose, that mission each day, we need to get rid of distraction.

When envisioning a future, purpose is primary. If our purpose is to perpetuate conspicuous materialism, then the production of 'stuff' needs to continue with everything being temporary, throwaway, replaceable in a short time frame. If on the other hand, our purpose is celebration of our human role as transmitters of cosmic creative energies, then the production of material things should be viewed as necessary distraction. Design and construction should be with long-lasting, ritual purpose in mind. The three dimensional world is an instrument through which multidimensional realities are accessed. These two conceptions of material reality are very different. One calls forth the corporate market economies that currently exist. The other stimulates new visions of some very ancient notions: the Galactic Village; the Agricultural City; the Sacred City; basically, humans living in unity with each other and in harmony with all other beings, living fully, everyone's needs, rather than wants, taken care of, so that there is time to focus on celebration, attunement, being Total Energy-bodies in a consciously galactic dance.

How we do it is to collectively envision our needs for food, shelter and clothing, for being together as a species, for total interactions with all other species. Then set about building this different way. Organize direction and discipline right in the middle of urban sprawl. Daily 'be' who we know that we are capable of being. Start small, on local scale. Start with one other person, then several, then many.

Considerations in decision-making based on Part XI

1. We decide the quality and content of our future.
2. A fully resonate world should be our goal.
3. As humans we have capabilities of living as Total Energy-bodies, interactively.
4. Each of us is a potential leader.
5. We can lead transitional lives attuned to cosmic change.

Part XII
PRINCIPLES OF STORY

A Catechism for the Children of De-Light

What Is Implied In Your Story?

Each person is a storyteller. We experience. We process our experiences, the stuff of thoughts and memories, as extremely complex brain patterns. Uniquely among Earthlings we communicate our stories in the presence of controlled, intentionally set, FIRE. Fires have, for eons, brightly burned at the centers of our circles.

If we were isolated individuals our stories would not be possible. For to understand, to think our experiences, we use languages which are based in culture. We are born into a way of using words. Our cultural upbringing shapes the contexts holding our experiential stories. Complexity of context is language dependent. What we say and how we say it requires, and is based out of, cultural heritage.

Stories of Total Energy-body experiences often involve dimensional interactions that are more easily understood in a language which intentionally codifies those kinds of experiences. The ancient Mayan used *ge* as the beginning syllable of words that referred to secrets of sacred interrelationships: zero, egg, essence, aura, Milky Way, and much more (Hunbatz Men, 1990). Growing up with a sensibility that words themselves mirror and effect continual creation is but one of the characteristics that distinguishes indigenous pagan peoples. Another is the notion that stories themselves are retellings. An individual cannot create an original fiction. All stories are of characters and situations that are part of much larger historical/ecological/cosmic contexts. We are always immersed within and never separate from these stories that disclose the continual nature of creation. In Gaelic the *aois dana* or gifted people are chroniclers of history, important events, lineage, and stories deemed necessary for survival. Specific storytelling training is passed down through generations. Stories are told when circumstances warrant: births, courtships, hunting and harvest, consumption, destruction, battles (human and other entities) and deaths. Stories allow the Total Energy-body of a community of humans to be revealed. In all pagan stories, from all indigenous cultures, interrelatedness of beings within All dimensional realities are focused. Attempts to disrupt or disjoin those primary relationships result in severe consequences. Hubris, or the arrogance that a person displays when they think they know better, is always recognized as dangerous.

In *Philosophical Investigations* Ludwig Wittgenstein states, "And to imagine a language means to imagine a form of life." The most primal languages sound like *calls* or *commands*. What we mean as we speak words reflects how we use words. Birds, Whales and Dolphins, Wolves and Cats all use their languages in the same way. When we story-tell we are calling an event into existence and we are forming or giving direction.

We are often not aware of the complex contextual nature of our stories, especially as we take a vacation from Total Energy-body interactions during the industrial-technological holiday. Cosmic stories are presented to worshipers a few hours each Sunday. Most stories are seen as entertainments, amusements, engagements to fill time rather than gain insight and teaching. Most modern stories reflect cultural breakdown. Heroes are those whose weapons allow for status quo dominance to be maintained. To be a storyteller in our era is usually not recognized as a shamanistic position. Stories in our time are for the most part not aimed at healing. The great exception appears to be children's stories. However, rather than teaching species and dimensional interrelatedness, many of these fantasies anthropomorphize all characters, making them simply reflections of human folly. Learning from trees, deer, pigs, is quite different from having them speak dominant culture values, participate in dominant culture rituals.

Dream stories are crucial to understanding Total Energy-body relationships in pagan cultures. Dreams in the dominant culture, if dealt with at all, are relegated to therapy. Because dreams and fantasies integrate dimensional reality shifting, unrecognized as 'real' by dominant-culture-advocates, neither of these categories of storytelling are rehearsed daily with both children and adults.

A Catechism for the Children of De-Light

And without practice in recalling the stories given in these experiences we forget how important they can be. Pagan cultures tend to spend attention time each day sharing what is learned while journeying dimensionally. Stories of these quests, visions, out-of-body-flights are understood as channels through which clarity from other dimensions is offered. This information becomes vital in daily decision-making, for it contributes a level of wisdom that is otherwise unavailable.

As speakers of Total Energy-body experiences our stories convey cosmic dimension. Gods, goddesses, angels, guides, ancestors, fairies, mountains, rocks, streams, all species of animals, plants, microorganisms speak through us. As storytellers we are channels for vast perceivings that are other than human. These characters are not simply symbols. They are more like emblems, representing pictorially whole lineages of Kin. Our experiences unfold within the situations enacted by the vast array of Total Energy-bodies different from our own.

It might seem incredible that so much complexity could be embedded within our stories. Because we tend to think of our experiences in a linear manner, the drudgery of one-dimensional living, stories that reflect only surface material world interactions, miss the De-Light that comes within interactions on myriad of dimensions simultaneously. Life, engaged from within a strictly materialistic perceiving, may will attempt to replace dimensional realities with jokes or fears of unknown or demonized realities.

If we consider all human communication as story telling, then no format is outside of the potential fullness and limits implied in story. Neither sacred books nor science are more or less apt as a way of speaking of human understanding. It is the particular context—science, religion, art, Total Energy-body, (or realities that encompass fewer dimensions)—that shapes the story. Listen how we 'tell.' It reveals the teller, his or her cultural base and the complexity or lack thereof, of the world being conveyed.

In Part II of this Catechism correspondence and reflection were considered. Every story consists of characters 'acting' in a variety of situations. How these character-situations agree or disagree with the listener's perceivings and recognitions in your story determines their attention and capability to actually hear what you are saying. A child whose experience and language skills are nothing like those of an adult hears only tonal noise when adult stories are told. Good storytellers realize this. Many pagan stories are therefore built around characters which any young person can recognize such as animals, birds, water-creatures. Situations may be unfamiliar to the child listener, but what will be initially remembered is character. These characters then become cultural emblems, recognized throughout a human storytelling life as representing or identifying a community's understanding. The same story told by different clans or religious sects is acknowledged as belonging to that people's story tradition. Or, it is said to be a variation from some other cultural group often because the character emblems are slightly different. Examples are many: Coyote in his many different indigenous American personalities, Shiva who is very much Dionysus and perhaps Kokopelli as well as other god-characters whose phallus symbolizes life-giving.

Any story you tell reveals agreements you hold with your culture(s). That culture continues to reflect for you a cosmic/earth view. Highly 'educated' Suburban Nomads living the edges of industrial-technology yet embracing pagan indigenous cultures, speak with forked reflections. We are consumers, yet we sound in our stories like we would prefer to live in primal harmony with all Kin. Our stories do not therefore ring true to the few peoples who have not adopted consumption as their major action. Stories correspond to how we actually BE in our world, or they are lies. Our stories can become commodities to be sold to each other, but their effect is to perpetuate dominant culture with a twist. If we stop industrial consumption, our stories will drastically change. They will not be printed and sold, nor will they ride the internet around the world. Most likely our stories will be enacted as some form of daily celebration of constant creation and De-Light.

A Catechism for the Children of De-Light

Stories are themselves vibrations coming from within our Total Energy-bodies. In Part III we discussed rapid oscillations setting up tensions where sudden releases are the continual creation of De-Light oriented life. The kinds of characters and situations in a story determine how it resonates. Stories coming from a violent, confused, consumptive society will have that tonal feeling. In fact without that feeling, it is likely that most people would simply reject them. To change our stories means to change our Total Energy-body life resonance. This is possible. It is even possible within an overwhelming or dominant consumptive social order. It probably means somehow existing outside that prevailing set of habits.

The 'vibes' within a story come from the story telling/story tellers, be they one person or a group of actors. But story resonance also resides in the way characters interact and circumstances develop. All stories hold interest through strategies of tension. Usually excitement is maintained through having characters confront obstacles. The internal power of the character is manifested through risk, how much he/she wants or is willing to endure to overcome whatever hinders a goal or destiny. Listen to yourself as you tell your own stories. Listen to others, to scripts on TV or in movies, plays, novels and poetry. Almost always you will hear this scenario, character taking risks to obtain something or bring about a change of situation. The vibratory quality of this ritualistic pattern is one of suspense for the listener. That resonance changes as the action is accomplished or fails. To the extent that humans identify with character situations of all kinds we share their Total Energy involvements. We learn their resonances, for a time possibly making them our own, depending upon the intensity of story. This is particularly the case in our dream stories. But it is the goal of every artist/story teller to create suspension, to set up alternate resonances.

When we understand that characters and situations are energy fields interacting with themselves and with audience/participants, it makes storytelling less abstract. In fact as we speak stories we speak into form, we create resonant life. Therefore, story telling, our primary human activity aside from innocent experiences leading to discoveries, is primary ongoing creation. We vibrationally set up our worlds. Story patterns release us or lock us in. Stories heal or they destroy. When we continually repeat stories of 'bummers' or 'downers' our vibratory world begins to be one of lowered, trapped, victimized resonances. These vibes feel like vortexes sucking from life rather than creating it. On the other hand, if we continually celebrate life, enjoying all the moments of experience, seeking fulfillment in complexity, then we experience vibratory joy, De-Light.

All stories imply polarities, contraries, ongoing change. The nature of energy itself is polar, interactive, always moving (see Part IV). Characters, whether they are fictional or 'real' are themselves representative of interactive differences, extremes, inconsistencies. The most interesting characters exude very active 'inner' lives, which often put them into conflict with the greater world around them, specifically with other characters who themselves have very different beliefs, commitments. Even gods/goddesses, cultural heroes/heroines, angels, ancestors, fairies, animals and all inanimate beings such as mountains, waterfalls, etc. have interacting individual polarities which produce their peculiar resonances. Without polarities there would be no resonant world. Those who speculate and try to live as though differences, diversities don't matter, miss out on life essence.

The most interesting stories contain measured paradox. Characters who function in apparent contradiction, inconsistency, illogic or absurdity tell us more about our complex natures than we think we know. As we tell personal stories we reveal these conflicting parts of our Total Energy beings for those who can see or hear. Laughter, outwardly showing our involvement with De-Light, accompanies the shear joy in appreciating how intricately ridiculous we humans are.

All stories exude rhythm. They are measured. Some stories flow like mountain streams, noisily crashing toward some far off sea. Some are quiet but move like mature rivers. Some are more like the oceans, settled in cosmically attuned beats. A story's rhythms betray its cultural source. They also convey the teller's excitement/resonance. A laid-back storytelling is usually not listened-to in the same way a story filled with tension and release is heard. The latter seems closer to moment to moment continual creation. The rhythm of a story colors the momentary frameworks into which it is being told.

In Part V rhythm is shown to come or be-within cycle. Cycles are signs of cosmic ordering. Many pagan stories reflect greater than human cycles. Some contain the energy of different Moons as they recur season upon season. Some stories are to be told only in a particular season, or when a planet like Venus is in a particular position, once every eight years. Some stories celebrate human interactions on a particular day or week, be they discoveries, warfare, births/deaths, achievements of all kinds. Usually the structure and the 'beat' of these stories mirrors their content and their timing in greater cycles.

Many of the stories of the dominant culture and many pagan stories imply causality. They are problem-solving puzzles. All our mystery, suspense, romance and adventure tales set up situations, which end in consequences. These linear plots give satisfaction to the listener/viewer when the problem is 'solved.'

Other stories do not imply causal logic. Two events causally unrelated but happening simultaneously (or seeming to happen simultaneously) can elicit meaning for those who are attuned synchronistically (see Part VI). Jealousy in a triadic relationship can become the basis of brutal interactions while mysteriously the Great Flood rises to overcome everyone who does not escape. Gods and Goddesses playing in the heavens notice humans on Earth doing quite similar actions. The human damming of swiftly flowing rivers happens to coincide with blockage of human arteries and heart disease. There are in pagan cultures story upon story, which imply interrelationship between processes, but function with a logic that defies critical, causal, analysis.

A Catechism for the Children of De-Light

Every story implies gender but beyond these male/female characteristics, and forming the core of many pagan stories, legends and mythologies, are androgynous characters (see Part VII). Having Total Energy-body balance in fact implies electrical/magnetic charges nearly equalized. The characters in many pagan stories hold this quality. Animal People, Ancestors, Angels and Fairies, all have this potential depending on the sexual viewpoint of the storyteller. Sexual differentiation, however, remains the basic identifying characteristic of most story characters. Story themes of love/hate, acceptance/jealousy, discovery/revenge, etc. are usually plotted between sexes. It is said that in contemporary dominant culture almost seventy percent of our popular stories can be classed as romances. Whatever story we tell about our own lives or those of others will be viewed and heard along gender lines. Comedy very often makes use of confusion or crossing of gender expectations. How Total Energy-body interactions reflect gender is the celebration that is basic to continual creation, De-Light, and is why much of pagan artwork of all kinds is deemed offensive to an orthodoxy which makes futile attempts to have power over sexual drives, attractions, male/female attentions. Gender is at once our most basic, primal way of critically evaluating, and our most revolutionary potential for continually birthing our potentials.

Every story implies direction. We convey our sense of place on Earth and in the dimensional universe as we tell our tales. Many pagan stories are of quests. Whether it is the Grail, Ancestor Spirits, or unity with all Total Energy-bodies in cosmic resonance, questing reveals our sense of orientation. Direction, way, path, tenor, places our story within culturally recognizable climates.

Every story reveals the teller's understanding of the complexity of dimensional realities. Most modern stories are like interactions between blocks of wood, clashes that show surface confrontations and winner/loser formats. Stories, in which characters engage and change emotionally, psychologically, spiritually, have "depth."

A Catechism for the Children of De-Light

Their dimensional characteristics tap our intelligence and emotional balance, bringing to life more of our total beings. Those stories which have character interactions, that involve beings and awarenesses of total universal resonant possibilities/probabilities, refocus our attentions toward resonant Kinships. We are more than biological/chemical/physical/psychological, beings. Stories which show us our greatness within Total resonance reflect our incredible, magical, capabilities.

The principles of relationship in Part X of this catechism show that any story we tell reflects how we understand the dynamics of power. My favorite examples are those which come from academics and 'do-gooders.' Telling stories of situations which are out-of-balance in settings which are themselves intentionally out-of-balance—such as conferences in expensive hotels underwritten by grants from corporate profits—while speaking as-if balance is the primary concern, betrays the luxury of dominance. Power in such a situation resides in comfort, consumption, in playing with "ideas." The tons of journal articles generated by such conferences are generally unread except by the few who share the position of dominance. Making decisions on crucial cultural/environmental situations —the story-subjects of these conferences of concern—would require the abandoning of such conferences and journals, in short, the whole privileged lifestyle that is academia.

Stories are entertaining, give pleasure, because of shifts in power equations between characters. Whether you are reading a novel, watching a thriller on television, or sobbing during a romance, what is most interesting to humans is how humans treat each other. Power is shown in relationships in many ways: Potency, ascendancy, control, authority, force, seeming omnipotence, all attract the attention of popular dominant culture advocates. Even in the stories from pagan cultures some of these excessive masculine tendencies seem very prominent, betraying the patriarchal bias present among all humans for the last 5,000 years.

A Catechism for the Children of De-Light

Stories coming from a more feminine viewpoint emphasize unity, harmony, working in the collective, being in vibratory alignment with all species, all life. These stories convey sharing, nurturing, caring, and generally relate power as fusion with others rather than dominance or use of others. Most stories from a female perspective remain unwritten. Writing stories, like taking pictures, violates the nature of continual, moment to moment creative energy change so necessary for attentive attunement. Writing experiences tends to make history rather than primary experience sacred.

Finally, all stories imply a future. How we storytell reveals our prototype reality. If our stories are of materialistic contexts, full of violence, without the magic of more than human dimension, if they are male battles for ethical or unethical dominance, then that is the future reality conveyed as vision. As humans we tend to impose on our collective world whatever stories are commonly shared. Stories shape how we interact. If we believe guns and romantic love/sex is the basis for acting-out the complexity of human behaviors, then we will pass this concept along to generation after generation. **Humans do not live rationally; we enact what we believe to be our story.** In our highest selves we extract morality from the story and claim to live with truths. It is in attempting to corner what is 'right' and 'good' that we become rational. Living out our stories, be they scientifically based or based on prejudices regarding race, color, religion, species, gender, is more an expression of who we have become culturally than it is any rational sensibility. Rationality itself is an expression of stories passed through generations who have found that those stories provide a basis for comfort, power, even De-Light

HOW IS YOUR STORY TOLD?

The most primal form of human storytelling in a formal setting is with a small group around a FIRE. The central fire symbolically conveys Total Energy-body transmission. When we are giving of all we are, when we are in resonant communion with all other life, we are ablaze, exuding enthusiasm, extending our Energy-body as a conflagration, inspiring participants to join in De-Light. Stories told with the intent of exalting while informing are so potent an event that celebrants rarely forget the experience.

All stories spoken daily as we relive immediate experiences, through all kinds of languages, can be inspiring. They can just as easily be depressing. It depends upon the outlook of the story-teller who must sense the contextual viewpoints of listeners and move them without frightening them. If your story is coming from too foreign a panorama, it many not be heard. Another story, that the listener interjects, that they make up themselves, might be happening in the gap between teller and listener.

The best stories are often based in what the dominant culture considers a lie. There is an immediate sense of tension when a story affirms a listener's sense of what is actually happening in daily life as opposed to what is said to be the norm. A lie is told with the intent of moving someone. It is ironic that slightly twisting expected reality releases the creative, frees us to soar in dimensional realms where all kinds of seemingly magical transformations can take place.

Characters in our stories must be capable of transfigurations, metamorphosis, transmutations, in short shapeshifting. Why? Because to express dimensional realities we cannot be trapped by imposed limitations. Obstacles must be worthy of challenge by heroes and heroines who know and use the powers of intention, attention, energy dynamics. For this reason dissonance and displacement are very important elements of dimensional storytelling for they signify abrupt changes of consciousness and Total Energy-body transferences.

Pagan stories may appear to follow critical rules of conflict, plot, character development, mimicking scenarios of dominant culture tales. But the intent is different. The teller is consciously loading each word, each sentence, so that the cumulative effect is overlays on top of overlays, culturally rich depths the annals of which reach back over orally remembered eons. While the story may sound like a transmission of tradition it is actually a welling-up of continual creation, De-Light. The firelight of this creative outpouring comes through the storyteller's eyes.

Each of us is a storyteller and as such we must be very careful what we speak as well as how we speak. For those trained in pagan traditions of perception, stories, be they personal or cultural, reveal all. There are no secrets; there is no place to hide. As a story unfolds so does the teller.

When we tell or act out the stories of others, the tellers and actors also reveal themselves, even as they take-on character. People who live in modern technological realities and who fly to conferences in large motels, where they wine, dine and speak of a paradigm shift toward unity with Gaia or Mother Earth, bespeak an obvious contradiction or lie. The karma of this hoax is seen in the newsspeak litany of daily disasters. We must always look to the total story, the complete context within which the telling is happening to see what is actually being spoken. When the actual gods worshipped are economic consumption and maintaining status among highly 'educated' peers, stories that claim affiliation with human ways that are outside consumption economics sound hollow. It is for this reason that a few indigenous peoples have isolated their communities awaiting the cyclic changes which will bring about an end of consumption for profit. Stories predicting what will happen when oil is used up, subtle chemical pollutants infect to a point where fertility damage threatens extinction, where the use of weaponry clearly wins no one power, have been passed through pagan cultures for eons. If these stories are alive within you, you tend to live without consumptive dependencies.

Some of our most interesting contemporary stories are of people who thrive on the edge of modern industrial living practices, using very carefully some technologies, but attempting to remain unattached. Many readers of this Catechism probably recognize themselves in this light. When we tell stories from this transitional condition, ask yourself, what are you saying if you look at the total context of your story and at your Total Energy-body relationships as the story reveals them?

A Catechism for the Children of De-Light

Our stories reveal our habits. Are there ways to change basic conventions, practices, usages within the expected conformity of dominance? Whenever we try to make these changes, will precedent prevail? Will the mental/emotional grooves cut by fifty years of corporate living and five hundred years of industrial disruption of all species communities in the name of availability fall to total-energy-body awareness? Can we isolate and rid our species of the energies that propel entropy?

Apparently focus on something, anything, is necessary for human sanity. Aware of this need, can we refocus our lives so that what we perceive as acceptable interactions are based upon totality? Or are we destined to remain a species isolated from all others, scattered in our fashionable frequencies? Wouldn't we rather live lives of total interactive celebration on a species and galactic scale? How we do that, how we experience and tell stories, in ways which reflect our adherence to multidimensional realities, is the twenty-first century challenge.

CAN WE SPEAK OUR WORLD INTO CREATION OR DESTRUCTION?

The power of human languages codified in story is enormous. The Holocaust performed by Arian Germanic peoples during World War II is but one tiny example of how a human fabrication can galvanize normal people to support genocidal acts. It is easy to create monsters, characters that embody all that is wrong with a society. It is equally easy for a culture to create justifications for aberrant behavior. Prejudicial stories result whenever contexts clash, as we pointed out in Part I. But stories are more than mental constructs. Most importantly they carry internally generated energy and the energies of those telling and retelling. When we open our mouths to speak, or we write what would be spoken, we are in transmission mode. We are broadcasting wave interactions. We are massaging those who are in receptor mode. If hate-filled, racist, images carrying enormous charges of focused energy gain status in collective consciousness, then all those, particularly the children, who are coming into agreements (and disagreements) with that social/cultural energy field will hold at least residue of potentially explosive predilections.

To maintain openness to all life interactions our stories cannot betray our preference as consumptive Earth-managers. Listening in the most all-embracing sense means that we take-in stories from all other species and dimensional points of view. We hear and create integration. This does not mean that our stories don't recognize that some beings, in sustaining themselves, may devour other beings. But we understand such transformations as the metamorphoses that they are.

WHO CAN WE TELL?

Those of us trained in pagan ways have been warned against expressing our experiences among those who defend the dominant culture. In effect, we live secret lives: Except when we recognize another person or species disciplined in the ways of Total Energy-body interactions. Then we can share what amounts to taboos in general society.

Those of us who are artists of various kinds can dip deep into our pagan awareness for source materials which we then shape in the direction of popular acceptance. In doing so we trust that we can lead humans away from consumptive arrogance toward interactive attunement to all life. We do not tell our stories easily. Often authorities shut down our productions, or they make it impossible to gain access to audiences. The literature and art and music that is chosen, century after century, to represent the dominant culture shuns openly pagan expressions, although within artistic forms, rhythms, and content you can recognize 'folk' ways. To boldly take on the dominant culture with carefully enunciated total-energy-body representations has never been advisable, and it may not be so as we begin the 21st century. But it is necessary. We need to bring daily human storytelling into harmony with momentary, intraspecies, energy-creative, universal life. Disharmony must be focused to show human shortcomings. This is a tall order given the urban nature of human lives, our false sense of consumptive comfort.

ARE ALL STORIES THE SAME?

Listen. Listen to all the stories that are told to you and around you each day. Most stories are of personal experience, revealing where the teller's attention lies. Most stories betray a reliance on consumer goods as the focus of life. Most stories are in fact based on experiences which are themselves fantasies generated by market economies. Listen. You will usually hear, within several minutes of a contemporary conversation in an industrialized country, references to movies, television shows, or radio rumors, as primary human concerns. People's actual experience of the world has become more and more one of interface with other stories. As we tell stories about how and what we experience in life we are actually telling about our encounters with other stories. This voyeurism is particularly present in the age of electronic media saturation. Collectively it keeps humans out of touch with personal Total Body Energies and with the continually accumulating energies of all of the rest of life.

The possible exception to this mediated communication condition is the stories told by elderly people. If you take time to listen to elders you hear repeated tales. These contain the lessons they have learned from decades of various kinds of awareness on Earth. All the luster of the corporeal comforts usually mellow or seem as major distractions when transition/death approaches. Even those people whose energy awareness is nonexistent tell of how very particular events shaped what they learned in this life. Bitching and moaning about continual pain reveals lessons learned.

Whenever possible we should seek out stories from those who are practicing dimensional energy interactions. Together our understandings of De-Light empower furtherance of these processes. Often we cross cultural and racial differences when we find others like ourselves. Pagan consciousness is very active all over Earth particularly when we leave industrialized urban plights.

A Catechism for the Children of De-Light

HOW CAN STORIES BRING US DE-LIGHT?

We need to generate stories and methods of story telling which activate all six senses. The closer a story telling experience comes to being a Total Energy-body occasion the more possible it is that participants will sense the fullness of creative outpouring.

Many stories passed through traditional indigenous cultures stimulate a kind of communal creativity. I've experienced the retelling of a very ancient native American story around a fire deep in the forest on traditional lands during which not only human participants but coyotes and owls and deer came, lent their energies, and made their presence known after the telling. We are not alone, as human individuals, or as human species. Every word we speak, every noise we make, every action we take is communication with a myriad of beings. In that telling the presences of human ancestors were also very prominently present. Beings outside the materialized dimensions are also called by Total Energy-body awareness stories. It is through these stories that the **commons** (a communal space outside of time) continues to live.

Stories that come from the sensibility of dynamic interactiveness in a vast cosmos of galactic swirls and a microscopic complement of the same, stories that are not limited by materialistic wants, greed, and human-centrism, stories that defy imposed dualism and linearity, even if they are intense, heavy, non-comical, bring our De-Light into a gathering of celebrants. For stories of continual creation among all creatures are constructions of future. We sense these stories will be passed along for seven generations and more. When stories are not from this vast cosmic commons, when they are *about* rather than *from*, then they are throwaway entertainments. Corporate stories, those that are acceptable to the dominant industrial/technical culture, skim along the surface, lack depth, or find their deepest moments in no more than human reactions. Such stories are products which perpetuate *want* rather than *need*, consumption rather than interactive sharing.

A Catechism for the Children of De-Light

Stories that embrace contraries and paradox while welling-up from cosmic depths teach us how powerful we are as moment to moment creation passes through us. Such stories can explode the moment in which they are told, being vibrationally as potent or more potent than primary in-the-moment interactions. The magnetic irresistibly of ancient prophecies exemplifies the potential all dimensional stories have to understand human responses to galactic/geologic patterns unfolding moment to moment within our immediate experiences.

IS OUR HUMAN FUTURE A RESULT OF OUR STORYTELLING?

As social/cultural beings we agree to retell our beliefs or habits. We also agree that stories that do not fit our popular awareness will not be retold, at least not in approved media. What becomes our history are very selected events that tend to align with whatever keeps the dominant cultural paradigm seeming real. The retelling of prehistory by anthropologists and archeologists during the last decade of the 20th century is a vivid example of how the Church and other economic interests have created a dark age where our knowledge of ancient cultures and their ways are concerned. Vast amounts of human experience have been lost due to cultural conquering, at least lost in the material sense. On a dimensional level we can access events of all times and places if we adjust our Total Energy-bodies to such resonances. When we make multidimensional adaptations often the information we receive shows us that conventional ways of interpreting 'reality' are prejudiced in favor of preservation of the current status quo. If that orthodoxy entails conquering nature for human comfort, then all stories in which humans are but one part of an interwoven commons where total awareness, rather than comfort, is the focus are deemed irrelevant, rebellious, seditious. The cult of the human individual in a hostile world is glorified. Stories expressing adventures of this individual are maintained as literature. These stories passed generation to generation train/

educate and become basic beliefs. Until their pattern is changed, dominant culture stories reign and limit the vision which informs human futures. Decisions are made within the limits of accepted stories, be they scientific, religious, or simply based in fears of the unknown.

So, is there any reality for humans? We can engage the energy of an immediate moment. Such engaging events have a reality that is different from that experienced when what we engage is our perception of an event in a moment which has just passed us by. When people ask, "is it real?," they are usually suggesting that what has just passed, some momentary event, hasn't lined up with their inherited prejudices of how the world should be. Outside human perceptions there are myriad realities. Whether we can understand these realities is a consequence of how large our worldview is, how we resonate with all others continually creating life.

Memory of past events becomes the fiction of a moment. That fiction can be so energetic that it overpowers all other realities or potential realities. Humans are collectively very good at living with fictions. Virtual reality experiences are rather new but only because the technologies associated with them are different than any previously experienced. It is necessary for human power brokers to keep as many people as possible living fictional lives to keep the industrial/technology/consumptive economy afloat. If agreements of a fictional nature were suddenly abandoned, in favor of resonance with the total life force and the commons, current economically based decision-making would seem foolish and a threat to survival. There is nothing wrong with fictional realities, but like plays or novels they should be dealt with as perceptions, especially when they are the basis for decision-making. Vital decisions about how humans interact with all other life should be made only in reference to Total Energy-body awareness with all other beings, all life forms, all energies.

We are entering a period of time according to many ancient cultural prophecies when great cyclic changes will purify the earth.

A Catechism for the Children of De-Light

Shivite, Tibetan, Mayan, Hopi, and other calculations point to the period around 2015 as a watershed. Change of monumental proportions will end the human materialization of this planet. Change can be fear-filled. Or it can be full of opportunities for expanding human capacities. The stories we carry with us into periods of galactic change, over which humans have no control, determine how we interrelate or react during the change time. During cusp periods ahead of great changes many smokescreens, in the forms of distracting stories, are broadcast by humans who attempt to exert control. Corporations speaking through their governments will/are creating destructive situations to keep people and their stories filled with fear. Meanwhile, on other dimensions, changes proceed that will modulate the effects of human consumption. The dynamic tensions/contradictions between what is happening outside human control and what humans wish to maintain will be the unfolding drama of the next several decades. Corporate/State/Military controls will become increasingly antithetical to nonhuman base realities, which will become more obvious. The existence of nations as we know them, the prominence of wealthy usurers, the dominant stories of orthodoxies will pale. Like all deaths this will be transformation. Those who survive will live very differently in a non-fossil-fuel-based world.

Trends show those who are alert that a cosmic scale metamorphosis is happening. Finding stories that elucidate that experience takes us across pagan cultures across the world. Incorporating those stories as mythos from which we operate is the job we are given as we make decisions which determine our collective human futures. Decisions are today being made for economic reasons in the framework of stories that suggest that human consumption is the base reality for which humans exist. Decisions about our futures cannot be made with economic/consumptive/greed as the focus. Rather we must know and practice the total energy interactiveness of the cellular commons. All our Kin must be involved in how we live. We can remain the arch villains of chaos in the universe, or we can decide to be the arbiters of beauty in consort with dynamics that are within and resonating around all life. The tension in our decisions as we leave the two-heart path and recover the one-heart way will bring us continual creation and De-Light.

WHAT COULD TOTAL ENERGY-BODY STORIES ACCOMPLISH?

Primary experiences, sensed moment to moment, totally unite a human with all other pulsing life. Sensitivity at this level has been relegated to saints, shamans, humans thought to be significantly different than most of us. But there is absolutely no reason why we cannot collectively drop the shields which bind us and keep us from total participation in the Energy-body universe into which we were born. There is no reason why, as great galactic cycles shift resonances, we cannot fulfill our resonant destinies.

Stories of our Total Energy-bodies need to be elevated to daily gossip, rumor, news. We, like many pagan beings who are not materially bound, need to practice methods of stimulating transmission and receiving experiences. This will unite all humans on this world with each other and with all other life beings. We learn to listen not only to our stories but those of birds, insects, four-leggeds and swimmers. We learn to hear and see from the perspectives of trees, grasses, streams, breath/atmosphere. We are not stuck in and on ourselves. The great value in this unity is that every moment is a stimulating challenge, a potential for being within creative life pulse.

Resonant unification through experience and storytelling of that experience does not do away with conflict. Conflict, confronting obstacles, rather becomes the stimulus for metamorphosis and continual transformation. Within the greater cosmic context, battles, collisions, antagonisms and hostility occur. They are spoken of in stories, but the attention to death and to the overpowering of one force by another is no longer emphasized. Rather both forces are resonant entities through which polarities are showcased and the storytelling of these events can teach how the continually changing universe works. Participants are exposed to the play of paradox and the potential for resonant unification.

Change as a priority moves humans away from pretensions of possession and status toward realizations of our place in creative flux: Effervescent, creative change, as the focus of our attention, moves us beyond ownership to continual concern for the commons. This does not mean non-investment in what is considered property. It means that our total energy selves care enough to merge with a place, a community, and all the creative outpourings that support lives of resonant energy. We are not speaking here of material world abandonment. Rather that world will function when fully resonating more like the dreamworld, more like 'the Garden' of ancient stories.

What is possible by changing the focus of our daily experiences/stories is nothing less than the creation of multidimensional environments which are lush with possibility, encouragement of all life forms, a kind of theatrical openness in which each being is recognized and seen in his/her resonance. In this place which results from how we tell our daily stories we will live ceremonially with all other life patterns, as children with an awe at our complexity and a De-Light that fills each day.

Considerations in decision-making based on Part XII

1. Recognize all elements in your story.
2. Total Energy-body stories are consciously different from those which entail consumer culture.
3. How you tell your story reveals the priorities you will use to make decisions.
4. We literally speak our human world into and out of existence.
5. We can tell our way into a totally interactive dynamic with all our planetary kin.

A Catechism for the Children of De-Light

Workshops, Seminars & Classes
relating to

A Catechism for the Children of De-Light
are available.

Contact the author at:
Touchstone Adventures
PO Box 177
Paw Paw, IL 60353
ph. 815-627-2716
or
6910 SW Plymouth Dr.
Corvallis, OR 97333
ph. 541-929-5782

For listings of other
Touchstone Adventure
books please contact
815-627-2716
or email: ajheim@carliving.com